Weathering the Storm

Weathering the Storm

The Financial Crisis and the EU Response

Volume I
Background and Origins of the Crisis

Javier Villar Burke

BEP BUSINESS EXPERT PRESS

Weathering the Storm: The Financial Crisis and the EU Response,
Volume I: Background and Origins of the Crisis

First published in 2017 by
Business Expert Press, LLC
222 East 46th Street, New York, NY 10017
www.businessexpertpress.com

ISBN-13: 978-1-63157-619-5 (paperback)
ISBN-13: 978-1-63157-620-1 (e-book)

Business Expert Press Finance and Financial Management Collection

Collection ISSN: 2331-0049 (print)
Collection ISSN: 2331-0057 (electronic)

Cover and interior design by Exeter Premedia Services Private Ltd.,
Chennai, India

First edition: 2017

10 9 8 7 6 5 4 3 2 1

Printed in the United States of America.

Abstract

Weathering the Storm explores the factors leading up to the recent global financial and economic crisis, how the crisis unfolded, and the response of European and national authorities. The book describes the rationale behind the measures undertaken to mitigate the consequences of the recession and to ensure that a similar situation does not happen again in the future.

In the wake of the crisis, various major changes continue to significantly affect the life and social organization of Europeans. For instance, a new ESM with a size financially comparable to that of the IMF was created; similarly, the reforms in economic governance imply much more intrusive participation of European countries in each other's macroeconomic policies. Moreover, the organization, regulation, and supervision of the financial sector have been drastically revamped.

The decisions taken by European and national authorities affect the daily lives of hundreds of millions of European citizens and countless more around the globe. An insightful read for anyone interested in understanding the topic and its effect on their lives, the book primarily addresses undergraduate students in their final year and graduate students in fields such as economics, finance, and political science. The main messages are explained through examples and charts. This first volume provides an overview of structure of the European financial system and of the origins of the financial crisis. The second volume focuses on the response given by national and European authorities.

Keywords

capital markets, economic and monetary union, economic governance, euro area, European Union, financial crisis, financial markets, financial regulation, financial stability, sovereign crisis, sovereign stability instruments

Contents

Disclaimer

The opinions and statements expressed in this book are strictly personal and cannot be attributed in any way to the European Commission.

Preface

The seed of this book was planted in early 2009 when I joined a group of colleagues providing presentations for groups visiting the European Commission. Many universities across Europe organize study visits to Brussels and the European institutions. It is not only universities, however, as groups of local authorities, entrepreneurs, and citizens also participate in similar study trips. Between 2009 and 2013, I had the chance of delivering over 20 such presentations to visitors to explain what the European institutions were doing to confront and overcome the crisis. The initial focus was on the rescuing of banks and countries confronted with financial difficulties. However, the messages evolved with the rapidly changing circumstances and broadened to include other subjects, such as ongoing policy reactions toward economic governance or the regulatory reform of financial services.

Speaking with these visitors highlighted the difficulties that citizens, whether they had an economic background or not, had in following and understanding the complex developments. While the circumstances leading to the crisis originated many years before and were built up over a long period of time, important decisions were taken in a matter of three or four years. The aim of these measures was to stabilize markets, to foster the capacity of the financial system to provide credit, and, ultimately, to establish the conditions for the creation of jobs and growth.

I thought that explaining the circumstances underlining these decisions, what they intend to achieve and what they entail was so important that it should be made available beyond the selected few who had the opportunity to visit Brussels, thus providing the impetus for this book.

I am very grateful for being able to have enjoyed the privilege of working for two of the main departments of the European Commission dealing with the response to the crisis—DG ECFIN and DG FISMA—while also following very closely the work of the third one—DG COMP. Therefore, I have tried to compile the views from those different perspectives from the lens of my own personal interpretation. Nevertheless, I sought to remain as objective as possible and to base my opinions on evidence. I have compiled a significant amount of data, presented mainly in a visual format, throughout the different chapters, as another key added value of this book.

Acknowledgments

I would like to thank the following colleagues and friends for their support and very useful comments in drafting the manuscript: Elemer Tertak, Stan Maes, Harald Stieber, Eleuterio Vallelado González, Carlos Garriga, Martin Spolc, Lars Boman, Matteo Salto, Victor Savin, Lucia Ribacchi, Gisele Hites, Toan Phan, Santosh Pandit, Miroslav Bozic, Manuel Thenard, Monika Nauduzaite, Rainer Wessely, Christian Engelen, Felix Karstens, Andrea Bomhoff, Stefan Pieters, Maurits Pino, and Francisco Espasandín Bustelo. Moreover, Jane Gimber, Caroline Simpson, Priscila Lee Burke González, Brenda Maher, and Stephen Curzon helped me with my ever-improvable English. Of course, any remaining errors are only my fault.

This book would not have been possible, however, without the hard work of many others. This is particularly true given the way decisions are taken in the EU with the collegiality approach of the Commission and the consensual method of Council and the European Parliament. This implies that decisions incorporate the contributions of many people and the views of many parties. While it is therefore impossible to mention all the colleagues from whom I have gained insight and with the risk of forgetting some important people, I would like to highlight a few individuals with whom I have most closely collaborated and gained valuable knowledge and support in my daily work and whose impact has ultimately contributed to making this book possible (in alphabetical order): Benjamin Angel, Markus Aspegren, Boris Augustinov, Alberto Bacchiega, Dilyara Bakhtieva, Nathalie de Basaldúa, Ugo Bassi, Leonie Bell, Andrea Beltramello, Álvaro Benzo, Alexandra Berketi, Sean Berrigan, Niall Bohan, Chris Bosma, Andreas Breitenfellner, Pamela Brumter-Coret, Alfonso Calles Sánchez, Nadia Calviño, Francesca Campolongo, Jessica Cariboni, Sarai Criado, Angela D'Elia, Lucía de Lorenzo Serrano, Miguel de la Mano, Ioana Diaconescu, Marie Donnay, Ann Sophie Dupont, Luis Fau, Leila Fernández Stembridge, Florence François-Poncet, Christophe Galand, María Teresa González Gómez, Carlos González

Maraval, Marie Carmen González Núñez, Lucas González Ojeda, Peter Grasmann, Gintaras Griksas, Óscar Gómez Lacalle, Anna Grochowska, Olivier Guersent, Jonathan Healy, Alexandra Hild, Alexandr Hobza, Anton Jevcak, Lukas Kaskarelis, Filip Keereman, Clemens Kerle, Ewa Klima, Daniel Kosicki, Anna Kozlowska, Nikolay Gertchev, Max Lange-heine, Zsuzsanna Lantos, Laurent Le Mouel, Agnes Le Thiec, Jung Duk Lichtenberger, Staffan Linden, Sarah Lynch, Mihai-Gheorghe Macovei, Alessandro Malchiodi, Maricruz Manzano, Martin Merlin, Michela Nardo, Mario Nava, Marco Petracco, Patrick Pearson, Ana María Sánchez Infante, Anne Schaedle, Dominique Scheerens, Felicia Stanescu, Irina Stoicescu, Triantafila Stratakis, Andreas Strohm, Gerda Symens, Michael Thiel, Gerassimos Thomas, Diego Valiante, Ivar van Hasselt, Erikos Velisaratos, André Verbanck, Rajko Vodovnik, Rainer Wichern, Markus Wintersteller and Alexandru Zeana.

An important part of the analysis presented here is based on data published by various authorities either at the national or the European level. I would like to thank the different statistical institutes and central banks, as well as their staff for their contribution, without which my understanding of how the economy works would have been much more limited. Similarly, the compilation of this public data would not have been possible without the collaboration of the many anonymous citizens and companies that have replied to surveys for statistical purposes.

PART A

Background

The structure and activities of the financial sector as well as the economic governance of a country affect citizens in their daily activities and throughout their entire lives: from receiving a monthly salary to the use of credit cards; from retirement endowments to the capacity of the State to invest in education and health. Many features of the financial system and economic governance underwent significant changes as a consequence of the crisis and subsequent policy decisions.

The European economy and its citizens will be bound by these decisions for many years to come. The new interconnections between the public accounts of the different EU countries can be mentioned as one example of the significant reshuffle in Europe's economic and social landscape that has been witnessed in the wake of the crisis. European countries have lent to each other—either bilaterally or by pooling their funding—unprecedented amounts of funds for as long as 30 or even 40 years. Historically, EU Member States have always been strongly dependent on each other through trade and other economic bounds. However, government budgets have never been so closely interconnected. Given the importance of public accounts for any country, this new state can act as a double-edged sword. It can provide a new push for deeper economic and social integration, increase trust among countries and eventually lead to a European State. However, it can also be the seed for increased tension and potentially lead to the breakdown and divorce of the European Union. Both citizens and political masters will have to decide which path they want to follow for the future of Europe.

The goal of this book is to provide an overview of the main features of the financial system in Europe, of European economic governance and how they have been impacted by the crisis itself and by the decisions taken by European and national authorities. In the last couple of years, a rise in discontent has been observed in many countries, in parallel with the development of new political parties with extreme views on both the right and left wing. Political decisions incorporate a strong component of social choice. This book provides information to citizens to help them understand the choices that were made and why. By providing comprehensive data and information, this book allows the reader to better understand the difficult circumstances surrounding those decisions so that they can build their own judgment about whether or not they would like their representatives to adjust the path in some areas.

Although much has already been written about the crisis, the strength of this book is to provide a helicopter view of the various dimensions, including a first-hand perspective of the actors involved in the decisions. While it would be difficult to recount this in minute detail, the book tries to go deep enough in each topic for the reader to get a clear understanding of the issues involved. The book can be seen as a starting point for understanding sometimes complex issues. There is a wealth of information that the reader can easily access to gain more in depth knowledge, starting from the references provided for each part.

I have focused on describing the circumstances and constraints, like data and information limitations, surrounding policy decisions. I have, therefore, avoided prescribing what should have been done differently, which might be easy to say with hindsight, but may not have been so obvious at the time the decision had to be taken. While the decisions taken during the crisis may have implications in the long run, they are not all set in stone. The European Union as a whole and other jurisdictions—the United Kingdom, Japan, the United States, the Financial Stability Board (FSB)—have all launched exercises to understand the cumulative impact of the regulatory reform put in place during the crisis. These exercises acknowledge that the difficult circumstances surrounding the decisions, the complexity of the financial system and the evolving environment[1] may warrant some adjustments in the legislative framework.

---

[1] The Goodhart's law or the Lucas critique indicate that any attempt to regulate (financial) markets affects the behavior of economic agents and, therefore, the previous frameworks and trends cannot be used as a benchmark for the effectiveness of the measure. In other words, financial regulation may require continuous adjustments. See also OECD (2016) and Arrow, Anderson, and Pines (1988).

A general idea of the structure of the European financial sectors, in terms of their size and how different segments interact with each other, is crucial for understanding the origins of the crisis and the reaction of public authorities in the various fronts. That is the focus of Chapter 1. The rest of the book is organized in five additional parts.

Part B provides an overview of *the origins of the financial crisis* by documenting how imbalances and risks led to the crisis. Thereafter, it explains how the crisis was triggered by the subprime segment in the United States and how it spread to other jurisdictions and sectors, including the doom loop of subdued economic growth, a weak financial sector, and stressed public accounts in Europe.

At the peak of the crisis and in order to avoid a widespread contagion and a meltdown of the economy, public authorities acted as a fire brigade by providing extensive emergency financial support. Thus, Part C (in Volume II), *supporting the financial system and sovereigns under financial stress*, explains and documents the financial support received by both financial institutions (e.g., bail out of banks by governments or the support provided by the European Central Bank) and governments (i.e., the use of the existing Balance of Payments facility and the creation of new instruments such as the European Stability Mechanism).

Besides providing emergency financial support to banks and governments, public authorities embarked on a comprehensive legislative reform agenda with the aim of making the financial sector more resilient and therefore avoiding the occurrence of similar crises in the future. Therefore, Part D, *the regulatory reform of the single market for financial services*, explains and puts into perspective the various legislative initiatives in a wide range of areas such as banking, supervision or consumer, and investor protection.

However, the reaction to the crisis was not limited to the financial sector. Part E, *macroeconomic policies: economic governance and growth*, covers the measures taken with respect to macroeconomic policies; in particular, the enhancement of the economic governance, which frames the macroeconomic interaction among EU countries. It also reviews the growth strategy and the measures taken with the aim of boosting jobs and growth in the European Union.

Finally, Part F, *summary and challenges ahead*, wraps up the information reviewed throughout previous chapters and presents the different strategic documents elaborated by the European institutions (e.g., the *Roadmap*). It places special emphasis on the vision for the future provided by the political masters of the European Union (e.g., the *Five president's report*) and the challenges that the European Union will have to confront in the coming years.[2]

---

[2] Latest developments: By the time this book was about to go to press, the UK referendum had just been held. Fifty-two percent of Britons voted for the United Kingdom to leave the European Union and triggered a period of high uncertainty. At this time, it is unclear whether and when the government and the Parliament will trigger the formal procedure to abandon the European Union (as established under Article 50 of the Treaty). These new circumstances make this book even more relevant as it provides background information to better understand some important implications of the potential future divorce and the many issues that will have to be negotiated. The financial support implicitly provided by the United Kingdom to Greece, Ireland, and Portugal through the EFSM (cf. Chapter 5) or the comprehensive EU regulatory framework of financial services which forms part of the British legislation (cf. Chapters 6 and 7) can be mentioned as two outstanding examples.

Moreover, while the weak position of some Italian banks was already under scrutiny, the uncertainty following the British referendum has also led to renewed pressure on Italian banks. However, circumstances are now very different from 2012. In particular, financial regulation is now much more constringent in terms of prudential requirements, additional limitations in the recourse to State aid and the need to apply the provisions enshrined in the new BRRD rules, in particular bail-in and burden sharing (cf. Chapters 6 and 7). A potential Italian program would have to comply with these new constrains or seek a waiver at the highest political level by invoking extraordinary circumstances.

CHAPTER 1

Understanding the European Financial System

Europe is comprised of a rich diversity of countries; however, one often becomes so familiar with national structures to the point of sometimes wrongly assuming that the reality is similar in the rest of Europe. The characteristics of mortgages and the use of bank accounts can be mentioned as two illustrative examples of the stark differences observed across countries.

In Spain and Ireland, virtually all mortgages are agreed with a rate that is adjusted to market conditions on an annual basis—using the Euribor or official rates as a reference. In countries like Belgium and Germany, however, the majority of mortgages are agreed with the interest rate fixed for as long as 10 years or even for the entire duration of the mortgage. The structure of mortgages and whether the rates are adjusted regularly or remain fixed for the entire life of the loan has an important impact on how risks are managed by banks across EU countries and on how movements in interest rates affect both the profitability of financial institutions and the capacity of households to consume and save.[3]

Similarly, one may have gotten so used to credit cards so as not to realize that, in a few European countries, up to 30 to 50 percent of the population did not have a bank account in 2011.[4] The access to a bank account and the lack thereof have important implications on how payments are organized, on how savings can be channeled to investments or on the possibility of using the Internet for online purchases.

---

[3] For further details, see Villar Burke (2016) or Garriga, Kydland, and Sustek (2016).
[4] See European Commission (2011).

These two examples illustrate how the European financial sector can be very different and much more complex than what we apprehend from our own experience in a single country. A broad understanding of the functioning of the European financial sector is the starting point to grasp the circumstances leading to the crisis, how the crisis unfolded and the constraints faced by public authorities to confront it. Moreover, a general idea of the structure of the financial sector, in terms of the relative size of the various market segments and how they interact with each other, is crucial for understanding the reaction to the crisis.

Therefore, this chapter sets the context for understanding the rest of the book and is organized as follows: it first discusses how funds circulate across the economy (Section 1.1) and the size of the different sectors in terms of financial assets and liabilities (Section 1.2). Thereafter, the various instruments or financial products are presented (Section 1.3) as well as the different channels: financial intermediation (Section 1.4), direct financing through capital markets (Section 1.5) and direct financing through alternative channels (Section 1.6). The complexity of the interconnections among the different sectors and the implications are discussed in Section 1.7. Finally, Section 1.8 concludes. The chapter is complemented by four boxes presenting the institutional framework of the European Union (Box 1.1), discussing the role of the public sector (Box 1.2), presenting the various financial instruments and their main features (Box 1.3) and discussing financial and economic bubbles (Box 1.4). To complement the perspective provided in the main text, an annex presents a summary of the circulation of funds from the perspective of fund flows.[5]

Box 1.1 The European Framework

This book is about the response provided to the financial crisis from a European perspective. It is therefore important to clarify some particularities about how the European Union is structured and organized.

---

[5] This chapter draws heavily on European Commission (2015).

The Conferral of Powers to the EU

A sovereign State can regulate and intervene in any domain. However, the EU is bound by the explicit conferral of powers enshrined in the EU Treaties. The European authorities can only act in the areas for which the Member States have explicitly transferred competences—for instance, monetary policy in the euro area has explicitly been transferred to the European Central Bank. In most cases, competences are only partially transferred to the EU and they are, therefore, shared between the Member States and the EU.

When the competences are shared, the exact functions of the EU and the Member States are guided by the principles of subsidiarity and proportionality. Subsidiarity indicates that decisions should be taken as close as possible to citizens—for instance, by local or national governments. In other words, EU initiatives have to demonstrate the need to act in common or that the objectives set out in the Treaty[6] cannot be achieved by only national actions. Proportionality means that no more than what is necessary to attain the objectives should be done at the supranational level.

A European directive sets out the principles and goals but allows Member States to define the means through the transposition of the directive into national legislation. A European regulation is directly applicable in all Member States and, therefore, it does not allow for a flexible adaptation to national specificities. Following the principle of proportionality, proposals for European regulations need to justify why a directive—or a recommendation—was considered insufficient to achieve the intended goals.

The foundations of the European project rely on a voluntary renunciation to sovereignty by the States, which is transferred, in specific areas, to the EU level. But this can only be done to achieve a benefit that needs to be accurately explained. Therefore, the principles

---

[6] The objectives of the EU are set in article 3 of the Treaty. In economic terms, the EU goal is to achieve an area of sustainable economic development aiming at full employment and social progress.

of subsidiarity and proportionality are critical for the legitimacy of the European construction and they rely heavily on the trust on the other partners. The relevance of these principles has become clear during the recent refugees crisis when many countries restored border controls and even built new fences and walls.

On top of the subsidiarity and proportionality tests, any European proposal must pass through the legislative procedure. Draft legislative initiatives are presented by the European Commission (which represents the overall interest of the European Union), which are eventually adopted by the Council of the EU (which represents the Member States) and the European Parliament (which represents the citizens). The Council and the Parliament, acting as colegislators, can modify the Commission proposals by including amendments.

While in most areas the European Parliament is on equal footing with the Council, in a few other areas, decisions are taken on a more intergovernmental fashion with a prominent role of the Council and a much limited involvement of the Parliament.

Economic Decisions in the European Commission: Main Departments

Among the three main institutions of the EU (the Commission, the Council, and the Parliament), the European Commission is, by far, the largest. It is therefore important to understand how the Commission is organized internally in the area of economic and financial affairs.

The reaction to crisis stemmed mainly from three departments: the Directorate-General of Economic and Financial Affairs (DG ECFIN), which is in charge of monitoring macroeconomic developments across European countries; the Directorate-General for Internal Markets and Services (DG MARKT, later restructured into the Directorate-General for Financial Stability, Financial Services and Capital Markets Union or DG FISMA), which is in charge of the regulatory framework of financial services; and the Directorate-General for Competition (DG COMP), which is in charge of ensuring compliance with competition rules. The role of DG COMP consisted in striking the right balance between avoiding the distortions of the government support provided to financial institutions and allowing for certain flexibility in the interpretation of State aid rules to accommodate the extraordinary circumstances stemming from the financial turmoil.

The Circulation of Funds in an Economy

An economy can be schematically represented through five institutional sectors with specific roles. *Corporations* produce the goods and services that *households* consume. At the same time, households provide corporations with a workforce and capital in exchange for the payment of an income, either in the form of a salary or a dividend. Some market failures prevent corporations from providing certain goods and services that are then provided by the *public sector*. Examples of such services include defense or the establishment and enforcement of the general legal framework.[7]

Moreover, a *financial sector* is needed not only for managing the payment system but also to channel funds from savers to investment opportunities. This is done through financial intermediation and maturity transformation. Finally, an economy interacts with other countries. While those other countries can also be divided into the same four institutional sectors (households, corporations, public sector, and financial sector), the external sector is usually taken altogether in a miscellaneous "*rest of the world*" category.

As can be deduced from the description of these sectors, they are all highly interdependent. As all economic sectors depend on each other, contagion through vicious and virtuous circles can multiply initial effects. Deep problems in one sector can be transmitted to other sectors and ultimately impact the whole economy. For instance, high unemployment rates can constrain the consumption capacity of households and therefore reduce corporations' income. Given their decreasing income, households and corporations may encounter difficulties to repay their credits to the financial sector. Subsequently, public finance can be eroded by declining

---

[7] See also Box 1.2.

taxes due to the reduction in economic activity and increasing expenditure in the social safety net. Problems can also originate, however, in other parts of the economy, such as in an unstable political system unable to steer the economy or in a weak financial sector struggling to provide credit.

On the other hand, a specific strong sector can be an anchor for a virtuous circle and lead the recovery of the whole economy to pull it out of a recession. For instance, a strong external sector can boost exports and employment, and a strong public sector can temporarily substitute the lack of investment by corporations and of demand by households.

The interdependence among institutional sectors stems from bilateral interactions between individual agents (Figure 1.1). In modern economies, any real operation—like the provision of labor, provision of capital, sale of a product or service—is generally matched with a monetary payment in the form of salaries, dividends, or cash. It is very rare, however,

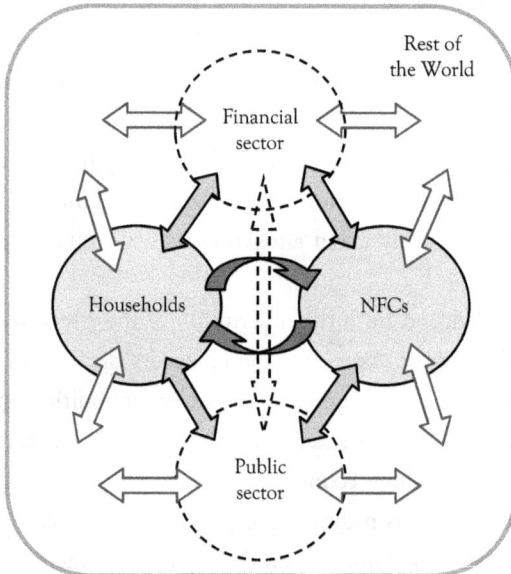

Figure 1.1 Economic sectors and interdependence

Any economy can be divided into four institutional sectors interconnected with each other and with the rest of the world.

Source: Own elaboration.

Note: NFCs: Nonfinancial corporations.

that there is a perfect match between the moment the real operation occurs and the moment of payment. In most cases, there is a certain time lag, which means that the real operations are translated into temporary financial positions between creditors and debtors. These positions represent the commitment to make or receive a payment in the future. Similarly, the institutional sectors can save in the present—by generating financial claims—to increase their resources available for future payments. In other words, financial positions represent an intertemporal transfer of resources between economic agents. They are recorded in the balance sheet of the sector providing the funding as a financial asset, and in the balance sheet of the sector receiving the funding as a financial liability. When, in the future, the borrower pays back its debt to the creditor, the respective positions in the corresponding balance sheets cancel each other.

Barter economies, and even economies based exclusively on cash transactions, have significant limitations. The flexibility in payments stemming from the existence of financial positions allows modern economies to achieve high levels of development. However, the existence of financial positions requires high levels of trust; in other words, one economic agent will be willing to accept a postponement in the payment if she can trust her counterpart will honor the debt in the future. Trust, therefore, is the cornerstone of modern economies. A clear example of this high level of trust is our reliance on banknotes and even electronic money as our regular means of payment.

Trust is somehow formalized or ensured by contracts, the rule of law and the legal system. However, trust is much broader and engraved in the values and culture of societies. Trust can evaporate even without formal changes in contracts or laws; this was for instance the case during the financial turmoil of September 2008 when confidence in financial markets fell. Excessive indebtedness or excessive inflation may also erode trust; yet, it is extremely difficult to discern the boundaries beyond which borrowing or increasing prices could become problematic.

In short, financial positions—that is, temporarily lending and borrowing—contribute to the well-functioning of an economy by enabling an enhanced mobilization and allocation of resources. At the same time, financial positions may also pose some risks as they rely on trust, which can suddenly drop. Knowing the dynamics of financing positions in an economy contributes to better understanding the functioning of that economy, but also to identifying where potential risk may be building up.

The financing positions of the different sectors in an economy, as well as the channels throughout which financing flows, are summarized in Figure 1.2. In broad terms, agents with an excess of financial resources (savers or investors) will provide funds to other agents with a financing need (borrowers). Two economic agents may directly agree with each other about the terms and conditions of a financial transaction, like an intercompany loan. Such operations are, however, embedded with several constraints such as negotiation costs and limited liquidity.

Capital markets may solve some of these problems by providing flexibility both to investors and borrowers. For instance, investors do not need to stick to the overall maturity of the initial contract as they can sell their investment in shares or bonds in the secondary market in case they need liquidity. On the other hand, capital markets enable borrowers to access a wide pool of investors.

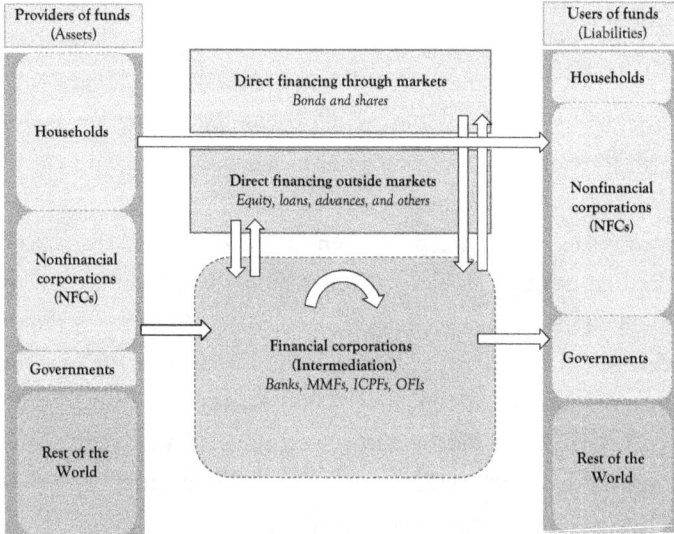

Figure 1.2 Circulation of funds in the economy: financing channels

Each institutional sector in the economy can provide and receive financing from other sectors. This can be done by the direct contact between two agents—sometimes using an organized market to meet—or through the intermediation of a financial institution.

Source: Own elaboration.

Notes: The height of each box is proportional to the actual size of the sector.

Nevertheless, not all financing needs and excess funds can be channeled and matched through direct interactions between agents or through financial markets. A household seeking to buy a house does not have the financial and technical capacity to issue securities in the markets. Moreover, most households and businesses do not have the capacity to assess the creditworthiness of a potential borrower. In this context, financial intermediaries provide additional flexibility in channeling funds from savers to borrowers by exerting two critical functions: maturity transformation and the assessment of the creditworthiness of potential borrowers. For instance, financial intermediation allows for a deposit placed by a household in a bank to be transformed into a mortgage to another household without a direct connection between the depositor and the mortgage borrower. In this context, financial intermediaries facilitate the mobilization of additional resources to be allocated to productive projects, which otherwise would remain idle.

Until now, we have seen that the existence of financial positions involves a provider of funds, a recipient, a channel, and an amount. Moreover, financial positions can take the form of different instruments, such as loans or bonds, with defined features in terms of maturity, repayment schedule and collateral, amongst others. The combination of these six main dimensions of financial positions—from whom, to whom, what, where, how, and how much (Table 1.1)—imply a dense network of bilateral relations. This chapter tries to disentangle the complexities of this network of interactions by quantifying and discussing the basic features of these various dimensions.

Box 1.2 The Role of the Public Sector

The main role of the public sector in an economy is to improve the allocation of resources and economic and social welfare. In general, an efficient allocation of resources can be achieved through market forces—that is, individuals acting in the pursuit of self-interest and meeting on a marketplace. However, a series of *market failures* prevent this to happen in many circumstances.

Table 1.1 Financial relations in an economy: dimensions

Who? Institutional sector	What? Instrument or product	Where? Geography	How much? Measurement
Households	Loans	European Union	Absolute terms (Euro)
Nonfinancial corporations (NFCs)	Bonds	Euro area	Relative terms
Governments	Quoted shares	Member States (28)	Percentage of GDP
Monetary and Financial Institutions (MFIs)	Unquoted shares		Percentage of balance sheet
Central banks	Deposits		Growth rates
Credit institutions	Ins. technical Reserves		
Money Market Funds (MMFs)	Other assets/liabilities		
Insurance Corporations and Pension Funds (ICPFs)	**How? Circulation of funds**	**When? Time**	**How much? Variable**
Insurance corporations (ICs)	Direct financing	Historical perspective	Stocks (outstanding volumes)
Pension Funds (PFs)	Through markets	Annual series	Flows
Other Financial Institutions (OFIs)	Outside markets	Monthly series	Gross issuances
Investment funds (IFs)	Financial intermediation		Redemptions
Financial Vehicle Corporations (FVCs)			Net issuances
Miscellaneous financial intermediaries			
Nonresidents (RoW)			

Data on financial relations are defined through a number of dimensions including the institutional sector, the type of product and the location, among others.

Source: Own elaboration.

In certain cases, not all the costs or benefits are incurred or enjoyed by the parties providing or receiving a service. These are the so-called externalities, which can be positive—for instance, public safety—or negative—for instance, pollution. Internalities or asymmetric information—for instance, moral hazard and adverse selection—the existence of public goods, coordination failures and market power or distortions of competition—for instance, natural monopoles, abuse of dominant position, cartels, reduced competition—are additional market failures which lead to an inefficient allocation of resources and loss of welfare.

A public authority can intervene in different ways to address these market failures. It can pass and enforce legislation which set the rules of the game seeking to keep the system honest—competition enforcement—it can also directly provide certain goods and services—for instance, education, health, or social protection—or it can use taxes and subsidies to internalize the externalities.

The public sector may also redistribute income to improve social welfare. Finally, it can implement macroeconomic interventions to overcome prolonged recessions and reduce unemployment. Indeed, the public sector plays a crucial role in smoothing the economic cycle by embarking in countercyclical policies, including automatic stabilizers. This is why it constitutes a cornerstone for an economy to address and overcome a crisis.

Economies evolve through recurring expansionary—contractionary cycles. Public finances help smooth these cycles by taxing profits during economic expansions and by providing social protection and not taxing losses during economic downturns (Figure B.1). These effects are usually referred to as automatic stabilisers.

In order not to run into problems during contractions, the public sector needs to save during the expansionary phase of the cycle. In other words, periods of economic expansions have to be used by the public sector to reduce its debt and get ready to confront the next crisis with sound public accounts. However, maintaining fiscal discipline is challenging. A public sector running surpluses usually receives pressure to transfer these extra resources back to the economy either by

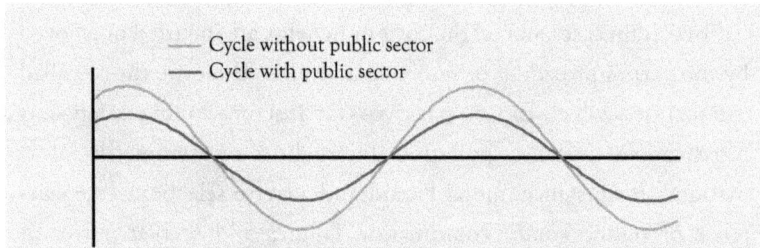

Figure B.1 The public sector and the economic cycle

The economy evolves in cycles. The intervention of a public sector contributes to smoothing the magnitude of the cycle.

Source: Own elaboration.

reducing taxes or by investing or spending those surpluses. Therefore, it is not always easy for a government to find the right balance between preparing for a future crisis—by reducing public debt—and supporting the economy during the expansionary phase of the cycle.

The Size of the Institutional Sectors

Total Positions: Assets and Liabilities

In 2015, the euro area economy had a total size, in terms of aggregated (financial) balance sheet of all institutional sectors, of more than €130,000 billion and more than 13 times annual GDP.[8] Between 2000 and 2015, the total financial position of euro area sectors more than doubled. This implies a much faster growth than nominal GDP, which only grew by 50 percent. As a consequence, the relative size of the financial positions with respect to the production—that is, the leverage—increased, particularly after 2005 (Figure 1.3).

---

[8] The analysis in this chapter focuses on the euro area; data for the EU 28 would provide a similar picture in terms of evolution and relative importance of the different sectors and products. However, there is a significant heterogeneity across individual countries; therefore, in a few cases, data for individual country are also provided. The European Commission (2015) provides additional details and analyses. Updated figures are published regularly by the ECB and Eurostat.

Financial assets

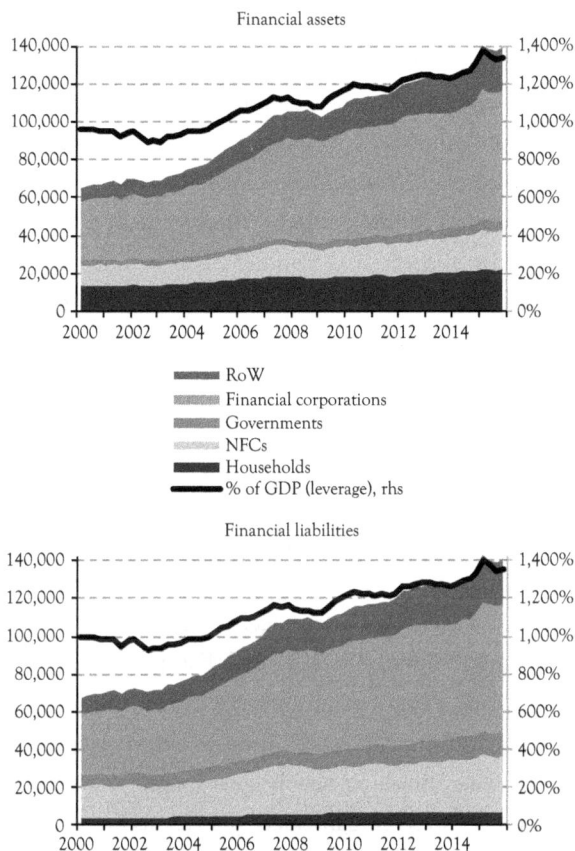

RoW
Financial corporations
Governments
NFCs
Households
% of GDP (leverage), rhs

Financial liabilities

Figure 1.3 Balance sheet of the institutional sectors, outstanding amounts, euro area, € billion

The institutional sectors have different sizes in terms of financial assets and liabilities. Overall, the total financing position (balance sheet) of euro area institutional sectors has expanded, particularly since 2004.

Source: ECB, Eurostat, and own calculations.

Notes: RoW: Rest of the world. Nonfinancial assets (such as buildings and machinery, land) are not reported.

Financial corporations represent about half of the financial assets and liabilities of the economy. Concerns have been raised about the potential excessive size of the banking system in Europe.[9] Although the relative size of the financial sector increased between 2000 and 2010, a slight decline

---

[9] See, for instance, Pagano et al. (2014).

can be observed thereafter. This is mainly explained by the process of deleveraging undertaken by banks in Europe.

Households and nonfinancial corporations (NFCs) represent about 15 percent of total financial assets each. Their joint relative size has significantly declined from representing almost 40 percent of the euro area economy in the early 2000s to about 30 percent in the last few years. The financial balance sheet of the public sector is much smaller. Finally, non-euro area residents contribute to the euro area economy by providing about 15 percent of financial assets and liabilities. These are mainly financial corporations from world financial centers such as the UK or the US; their relative importance has continuously expanded from representing about 10 percent in 2000 to more than 16 percent in 2015.

Following the outbreak of the crisis, a debate emerged about whether indebtedness or leverage had become excessive so as to negatively affect confidence. Several voices argued about the need to reduce the indebtedness of the different agents or "deleverage." Throughout the crisis, however, there were no signs to indicate such a trend. For instance, the 16th Geneva Report on the World Economy[10] argues that, despite the length and depth of the crisis, the world has not yet begun to deleverage; global debt-to-GDP is still growing, breaking new heights (page 1). The Geneva report also indicates that deleveraging interacts in a vicious loop with slow nominal growth, as the latter makes the deleveraging process harder and the former exacerbates the economic slowdown (page 2).[11] Eventually, according to the latest data, some signs of declining leverage seem to be emerging.

Net Financial Positions

The difference between financial assets and financial liabilities, or net financial worth, indicates the cumulative net contribution to the financing of the economy provided by each financial sector. When a sector has a positive net financial worth, it provides financing to other sectors. When net financing worth is negative, the sector is absorbing financing, in other words, it has a financing need to be covered by borrowing from other sectors.

---

[10] Buttiglione et al. (2014).

[11] Other authors arrive to similar conclusions, for instance, Roxburgh et al. (2012); Reinhart, Reinhart, and Rogoff (2015); or Stephanie and Rogoff (2015).

Households are the main provider of funding to the economy. Households' net savings represented more than 140 percent of GDP in 2015 and originated most of the financing created in the euro area economy throughout the crisis. Indeed, households' net financial worth increased from €10,500 billion in 2008 to almost €15,000 billion in 2015 (Figure 1.4). Financing ultimately coming from households also had to be used for compensating the withdrawal of funding resources by foreign investors, whose net positions significantly declined throughout the same period.

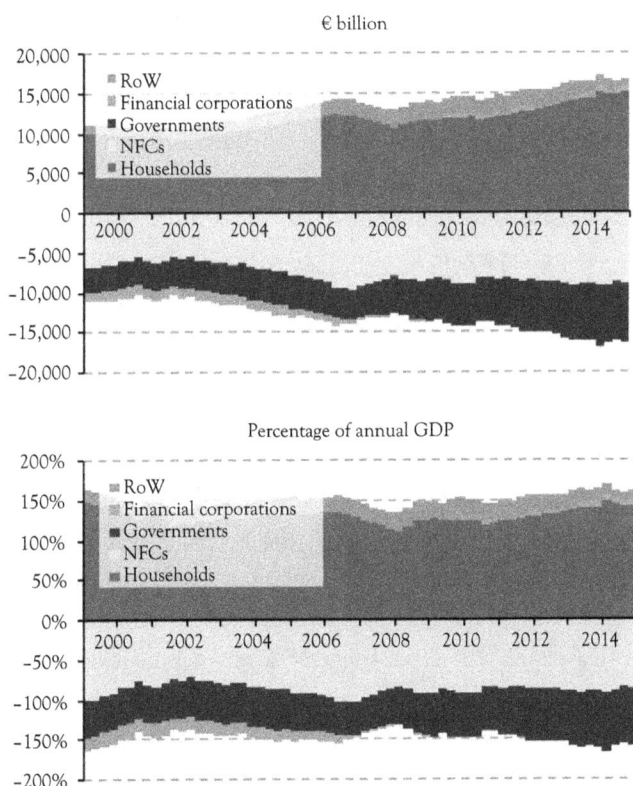

€ billion

Percentage of annual GDP

Figure 1.4 Net financial worth of the institutional sectors, outstanding amounts, euro area

The net financial worth of the institutional sectors is significantly smaller than gross financial positions. Households provide net funding to NFCs and governments. Despite its large size in terms of financial assets and liabilities, the net contribution of the financial sector to the financing of the economy is negligible. Net financial worth has expanded in absolute terms, but it has remained rather stable as a percentage of GDP.

Source: ECB, Eurostat, and own calculations.

Notes: RoW: Rest of the World. Net financial worth is computed as financial assets minus financial liabilities.

Nonetheless, two important factors have been eroding the capacity of households to continuously provide financing to the rest of the economy. In the short run, unacceptably high levels of unemployment entail a net absorption of financial resources. In the long run, demographic developments, including longer lives and reduced fertility rates, imply a shrinking share of working population with respect to number of people already in retirement.[12]

The main net users of financial resources are NFCs and governments. NFCs can obtain credit because they have large amounts of equity and significant amounts of tangible assets such as buildings, machinery, and others that are not accounted for in the financial accounts. Governments borrow against their future collection of taxes, their main source of revenues. The net financial worth of NFCs remained rather stable throughout the crisis.

The financial and economic crisis triggered important financing needs in the public sector. Government net financial negative worth (net public debt) increased from €4,000 billion in 2008 to over €7,000 billion in 2015. This is explained by its function as an automatic stabilizer—providing social benefits, for example[13]—but also for the need of the public sector to step in to support financial institutions under stress.

We have seen that the balance sheet of the financial sector represents about half of the aggregated balance sheet of the economy. However, given their intermediation function, the net contribution of financial corporations to the financing of the economy is only incidental.

The financing of the economy is completed by resources provided by the external sector. The crisis triggered a retrenchment of the financial sector to their main activities, including the reduction of cross border positions. Accordingly, the net lending obtained by the euro area from the rest of the world declined from a peak of more than 30 percent of GDP in 2009 to less than 10 per cent in 2015.[14]

---

[12] Unemployment is further discussed in Section 1.7 and demographic trends in Section 10.3.

[13] See Box 1.2.

[14] See European Commission (2015) for further details.

Box 1.3 The Financial Instruments Available in an Economy: An Overview

The provision of funding can be formalized through different instruments or products with specific features in terms of liquidity, maturity, or legal implications. Among the wide range of sources that are available for firms to finance their activities, a major divide appears between equity instruments and debt instruments. Obtaining funding through equity instruments implies the transfer of property to equity providers and their involvement in decision making. Consequently, the remuneration of equity depends on the results of the company. In other words, equity instruments are the first layer for the absorption of losses, but, in compensation for that, equity holders benefit from potential extraordinary profits.

In principle, equity instruments are permanent or perpetual, so holders need to find a buyer in case they want to untie their positions. In this context, *quoted shares* can be more easily liquidated than *other equity instruments* because they are quoted in organized markets. Note that equity includes both fresh injections of capital—either at the inception of a company or at a later stage—and the earnings retained throughout the life of the firm. This applies both to quoted shares and to other equity instruments. The case of *insurance technical reserves* represents a special case of equity.

Debt instruments do not transfer property and usually require a fixed interest payment[15] and the reimbursement of the principal within a specific time frame. *Bonds* are standardized debt instruments that are traded in organized markets. *Loans* are bilateral contracts, which cannot be traded unless they are converted into bonds through securitization. Besides borrowing from banks, firms can obtain *loans from other economic agents*. There are four types of such loans: first, loans agreed between two companies belonging to a group of companies,

---

[15] Although interest rates can also be linked to some market indexes, these variable interest rates are "fix" in the sense that they do not depend on the performance of the company.

also called intragroup lending; second, loans agreed between two companies not belonging to the same group, usually stemming from a supplier-customer relationship but that cannot be classified as trade credit; third, loans provided by households to entrepreneurs and small firms—often from family and friends; finally, loans provided by the State and public authorities, whether subsidized or not—for instance, stemming from a government initiative to promote entrepreneurs and start-ups.

The economic transactions between a company and its suppliers, clients, employees and other stakeholders imply intrinsic financing resources that cannot be provided by capital markets nor by the financial sector. These sources of funding are usually generated by the difference between a continuous accrual of economic value and a point-in-time nature of payments and settlements. Therefore, they are not formalized in the form of a loan contract. These sources of funding can be grouped in the category of *trade credit and advances* (receivable or payable), where trade credit refers to the financing positions within the supplier-customer chain and advances refers to the relations with other stakeholders.[16]

There are many examples of trade credit and advances. When we purchase plane tickets months before our actual journey through a webpage, we are providing an advance to the air carrier. In business-to-business relations it is very common to make the payment up to ninety days after the delivery of goods. Another example is a monthly salary: employees of a company generate value on a daily basis, but they only receive their wages on a monthly basis. Similarly, utility companies—like electricity, water, or Internet suppliers—provide their services on a continuous basis but they are only paid at the end of the period—once a month, for instance.

Taxes due and *tax claims* have similar features to advances. Companies intermediate in the collection of VAT taxes, which are only settled once a quarter. Income taxes, which are settled once a quarter

---

[16] The financial sector can in fact play a role in trade credit and advances by providing liquidity through factoring and other forms of asset-back lending.

or once a year, have somehow an analogous nature. When, following a tax declaration, one is entitled to a tax reimbursement, the household or the firm have been financing the State; similarly, when one is required to pay additional taxes, one has been financed by the State.

The label *derivatives* includes a wide range of instruments with the only commonality of being somehow linked to the evolution of an underlying asset. *Deposits and currency* are the most liquid instruments; they are usually kept for transactional purposes, although their holders may also receive a small remuneration.

In general, in order to guarantee the financial stability of an economic agent, long-term assets—such as buildings or machinery—should be financed by long-term sources of funding—such as equity, long-term loans or long-term bonds—and current assets—such as inventories or advances to customers—should be financed by a short-term source of funding.[17]

In any financial transaction, there are two counterparties involved: one providing the funds and the other one providing the needs. As a consequence, any instrument is recorded twice: as an asset by one counterpart and as a liability by the other. However, given the intermediation function of the financial sector, the correspondence between assets and liabilities can be complex.

Sources of Financing Used by the Economy: Instruments

The composition of assets within the nonfinancial sectors (households, NFCs and governments) provides an indication of how the economy is organized and the role of financial intermediation and the financial sector. If households keep their savings in the form of deposits, banks can intermediate and provide credit through loans. However, if households

---

[17] However, while individual components of current assets are changing continuously, there is a certain amount of such assets that remains in the balance sheet of the agent. This, usually known as working capital, should also be financed by long term liabilities.

prefer to directly invest in bonds or equity, there is little room for bank intermediation—and maybe even no need.

In general, the product mix depends on the "preferences" of economic agents. These preferences are in fact a combination of factors such as the need for liquidity for transactional purposes, the remuneration level of the different instruments, risk aversion or entrepreneurial culture, amongst others. Transaction costs, informational barriers or bankruptcy regimes may also play a role. In other words, they are strongly driven by legal and institutional frameworks.[18]

The funding mix differs widely from one sector to the other[19] (Figure 1.5). NFCs finance more than half of their activities with own resources (51 percent); the majority of which takes the form of equity other than quoted shares (35 percent total liabilities) and, the rest, the form of quoted shares (16 percent). Given that less than 0.05 percent of EU companies have listed shares,[20] a 16 percent use of quoted shares seems to signal well-developed equity markets (see Section 1.5).

NFCs use also a variety of debt instruments including bank loans (14 percent of total financing sources), other loans (18 percent), and trade credit and similar advances (11 percent of liabilities). The use of bonds (4 percent) and other financing sources (1.5 percent) is much more limited. Overall, NFCs obtain one third of their financing from the traditional financial sector—bank borrowing, bonds, and quoted shares—while the other two thirds come from alternative sources.

Households use bank loans as their main source of financing (77 percent of their financial liabilities), while the use of other sources is more limited.

The bulk of governments' financial liabilities are bonds (over 70 percent of their financial liabilities). Bank loans, other loans and "other sources"—such as trade credit, pending bills, pending transfers, and advanced taxes—represent about 10 percent each.

---

[18] See the work of Douglass C. North about institutions.

[19] The analysis presented here focuses exclusively on the liabilities side of the balance sheet. An overview of the mix of instruments in the assets side is available in European Commission (2015).

[20] There are over 22 million companies in the EU, but less than 9 thousand of them have listed shares.

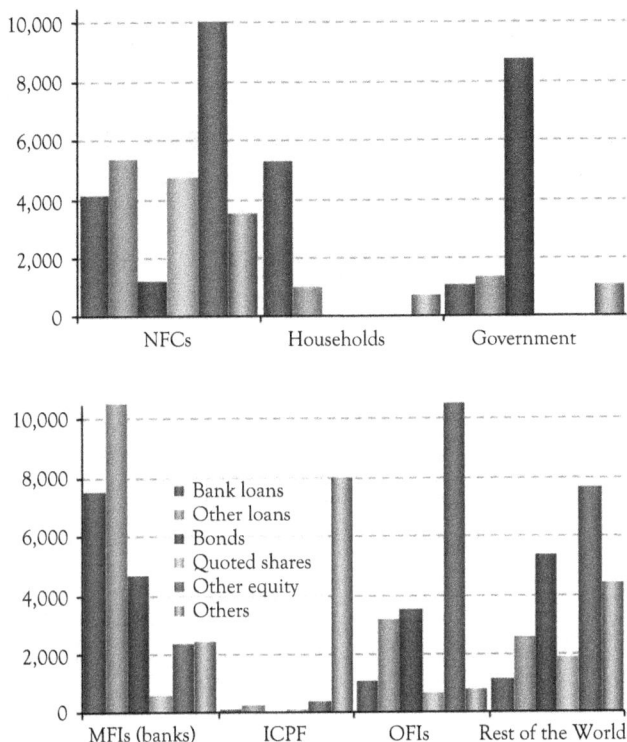

Figure 1.5 Sources of funding (financial liabilities), euro area, 2015, €billion

The funding mix differs across institutional sectors. Households use mainly bank loans and governments mainly bonds. On the other hand, NFCs, MFIs and OFIs use a variety of funding sources.

Source: Eurostat and ECB: euro area accounts.

Note: "Bank loans" for MFIs correspond to interbank deposits received. "Other loans" for MFIs correspond to deposit received (other than interbank): €14,700 billion. "Other equity" for OFIs: €16,300 billion. "Other financing" for ICPFs corresponds to insurance technical reserves. Investment fund shares and mutual fund shares are included in other equity.

The financial sector stands out due to the low level of equity issued in the market—only 2 percent of its financial liabilities are quoted shares compared to 16 percent for NFCs. Capitalization—including both quoted shares and other equity—is particularly low for banks—less than 10 percent of total liabilities compared to over 50 percent in the case of NFCs.[21] Even when the financial sector is taken as a whole, capitalization is rather

---

[21] See Kuehnhausen and Stieber (2014).

limited—less than 30 percent. Moreover, the interlinkages within the financial sectors—for instance, the equity of OFIs corresponds mainly to shares of investment funds and mutual funds[22]—should not be neglected. This implies a lower loss absorption capacity than that which the headline figure of equity may seem to suggest.[23] In the wake of the financial crisis and following both market pressure and regulatory reforms, the financial sector, and banks in particular, has been raising new capital to reinforce their loss absorption capacity; however, the financial sector still functions with much lower capital levels than NFCs.

The use of bonds as a source of funding is significant for banks (14 percent of financial liabilities) and OFIs (13 percent) and much less so for ICPFs (1 percent). The most prominent source of funding for banks are deposits and loans provided by other sectors (45 percent) and interbank lending (23 percent). These two categories are also somehow relevant for OFIs (a combined value of 18 percent). The main source of financing for ICPFs is insurance technical reserves—included in "Others."

Turning to the evolution of the funding mix,[24] the crisis particularly eroded the value of the equity of NFCs (both quoted shares and other equity) in 2008–2009, and to a slightly lesser extent the second dip of 2011 (Figure 1.6). This corresponds with the loss absorption function of equity. Equity other than quoted shares, however, recovered precrisis values already from mid-2010. The recovery in the value of quoted shares seems to have lagged behind. In 2015, the expansion in quoted shares and other equity seems to have ground to a halt, which already hints at the turmoil of early 2016.

---

[22] A number of authors argue that, in the last 10 to 15 years, there has been an increased intrafinancial system complexity via the lengthening of intermediation chains (see, for instance, Adrian and Shin 2010).

[23] In this context, capital requirements legislation includes a correction for intragroup holdings of equity as these have a much lower loss absorption capacity.

[24] The outstanding amounts of liabilities provide an overview of how the funding mix of the different institutional sectors evolves over time. However, the changes may correspond to actual increases or decreases or to valuation effects—for instance, changes in exchange rates affect debt nominated in foreign currency. An analysis of flows provides a complementary view by focusing on actual increases and decreases (see Annex 1.1).

Distribution of total liabilities

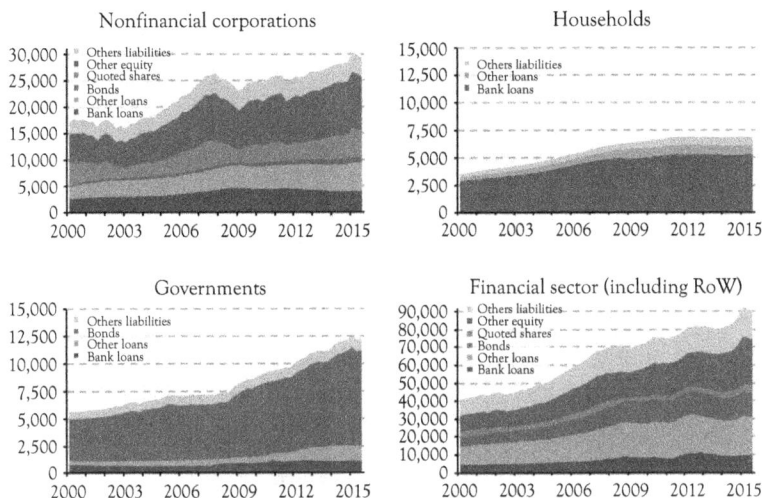

Individual series

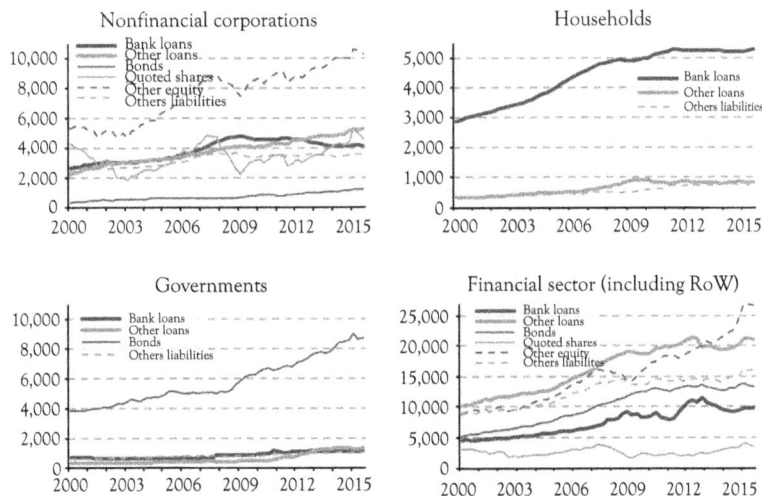

Figure 1.6 Sources of funding (financial liabilities), breakdown by instrument, euro area, € billion

A differentiated impact of the crisis is observed across sectors and sources of funding.

Source: ECB, Eurostat, and own calculations.

Notes: The financial sector includes MFIs, OFIs, and ICPFs. RoW: Rest of the World. Deposits received by banks are included under the category "Banks loans" (interbank deposits) or "Other loans" (deposits other than interbank). Investment fund shares and mutual fund shares are included in other equity.

A stagnating or even declining volume of bank loans to the nonfinancial part of the economy can be observed since the outbreak of the crisis. It has been argued that the capacity of the banks to provide loans has been jeopardized by the financial crisis; however, demand factors may also be playing a role.[25] A similar evolution is observed for other liabilities, consisting mainly of trade credit. This may be explained by the context of reduced economic activity (i.e., demand factors) and also, to a certain extent, by a certain decline in confidence observed since the outbreak of the crisis.

This negative evolution in loans and other liabilities is more than compensated by the expansion of bonds—mainly issued by governments but also by large NFCs—which almost doubled between 2008 and 2015 and of loans other than bank loans (intercompany loans, loans from households, and government loans), which increased by more than 40 percent during the same period.

Overall, and despite the crisis, the total size of funding resources used by the NFCs of the economy expanded between late 2007 and 2015 (from €40,000 billion to almost €50,000 billion). Although an important part of this expansion is explained by the increase in government debt (from €7,200 billion to €12,500 billion), NFCs also increased their use of funding to a certain extent (from €12,500 billion to €14,300 billion), but at a slower pace than in mid-2000.

Turning to the financial sector, the financial crisis negatively impacted all sources of financing, which in general stagnated or even started to decline from 2013. A notable exception is the significant expansion in "other equity," which is mainly explained by the expansion of OFIs—particularly investment funds. Since the outbreak of the crisis, the overall size of funding resources used by the financial sector has evolved in "waves" with periods of roughly two years of stagnation followed by about two years of expansion. This may be linked to the excessive size reached by the financial sector—with a total size of almost €90,000 billion[26] compared with about €10,200 billion of the euro area GDP—and recurring pres-

---

[25] See, for instance, Giovannini et al. (2015).

[26] This figure includes the "rest of the world," which, to a large extent, plays a similar role than the domestic financial sector.

sures to deleverage (cf. discussion in Section 1.2). Having said that, the different subsectors within the financial sector show divergent evolutions (see next section for further details).

Financial Intermediation

Once the different instruments that can be used to finance economic activities have been reviewed, we will look at the providers of those funding resources or financial channels. Therefore, this section focuses on the intermediation through financial institutions and the next two sections focus on the direct financing either through organized markets, or by the direct interaction between ultimate providers and end users of funds.

The Role of Financial Institutions

Financial institutions perform a number of functions such as creating and managing payment systems, providing market infrastructure—such as trading platforms or management of initial public offerings—providing savings facilities for households—for instance, investment funds, insurance or pension funds—participating actively in markets—for instance, through "proprietary trading" of bonds and quoted shares—providing liquidity—for instance, through factoring—and helping economic actors to manage and insure against risks—for instance, insurance companies and pension funds.

The intermediation function of the financial sector implies channeling savings and excess liquidity from one part of the economy toward other areas in need of funding. In general, however, financial institutions do not create net additional financial resources (see Section 1.3). Banks usually assess the risk of their clients and should only finance projects that they consider viable. The intermediation and risk assessment function of banks is usually combined with maturity transformation. This means that a bank will typically be financed through short-term savings—typically overnight deposits—and will provide long-term loans—for instance, for buying a house or for a factory to invest in equipment.

While the maturity transformation function of banks plays a crucial role in the financing cycle of the economy, it also puts banks in an inherently weak position. In light of the fact that they use short-term funding to finance long-term projects, they can be confronted with liquidity problems if a large share of depositors were to claim their funds at a given moment. To mitigate this risk, financial institutions must comply with some prudential requirements in terms of liquidity and capital. In addition to that, the central bank provides a lender of last resort safety net in the event of liquidity constraints.

If a bank were to act recklessly, public authorities could be confronted with a dilemma between the risk that basic financial services, such as ensuring the functioning of the payment system, could collapse, and bailing out banks with a reckless behavior. An exploitation of this dilemma by banks is known as moral hazard.

A moral hazard situation appears when the potential benefits and risks are not well balanced or do not fall on the same actors. This is for instance the case of an insurance contract, which leads a person to be less careful in her behavior because she knows that the potential damages will be covered by the insurance company.

While it is not possible to completely eliminate moral hazard, prudential requirements and supervision of financial institutions tries to strike a balance between private initiative and maintaining financial stability. The crisis has shown that the previous framework was not properly calibrated. A series of measures has been implemented to better constrain the occurrence of moral hazard situations (see Part D).

Subsectors of Financial Intermediation: Size and Evolution

Financial institutions can be classified in three subsectors: monetary financial institutions (MFIs), insurance corporations and pension funds (ICPFs), and other financial institutions (OFIs). In 2015, MFIs' total assets accounted for about half of all euro area financial institutions, ICPFs for about 15 percent and OFIs for about 40 percent. MFIs can further be split into credit institutions, money market funds and the central bank; OFIs, can be split into investment funds, financial vehicle corporations and miscellaneous financial intermediaries; ICPFs can be split into insurance corporations and pension funds (Figure 1.7).

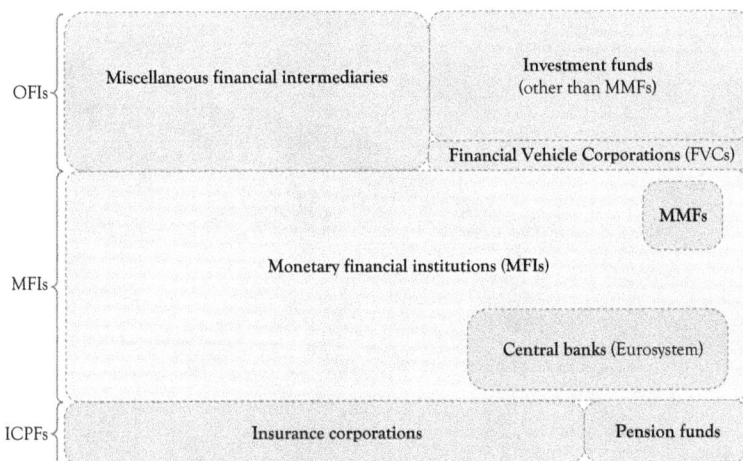

Figure 1.7 Financial intermediaries and subsectors

Source: Own elaboration.

Notes: The surface of each box is proportional to the size of the sector in the euro area in 2015. OFIs: Other financial institutions. MFIs: Monetary financial institutions (credit institutions, MMFs and central banks). MMFs: Money market funds. ICPFs: Insurance corporations and pension funds.

In 2015, the total balance sheet of euro area financial institutions was almost €70,000 billion, over six times the annual GDP of the euro area. Between the early 2000s and 2012, euro area financial institutions doubled in size (in terms of total assets). This was driven by growth in all the three main subsectors. Since the onset of the crisis, however, the banking sector grew much slower than the other sectors, and even declined in size after 2012. On the other hand, both ICPFs and OFIs kept expanding, particularly the latter (Figure 1.8). While a part of this growth may be autonomous, it has also been driven, to a large extent, by a transfer of assets from banks to OFIs. Indeed, it has been argued that the increasing regulatory requirements imposed on banks and the pressure to deleverage have led to a transfer of assets to other less regulated parts of the financial system, the so-called shadow banking sector.[27] If that would be the case, while the banking sector may seem smaller, the overall size of the financial

---

[27] See FSB (2015).

€ billion

Distribution, percentage

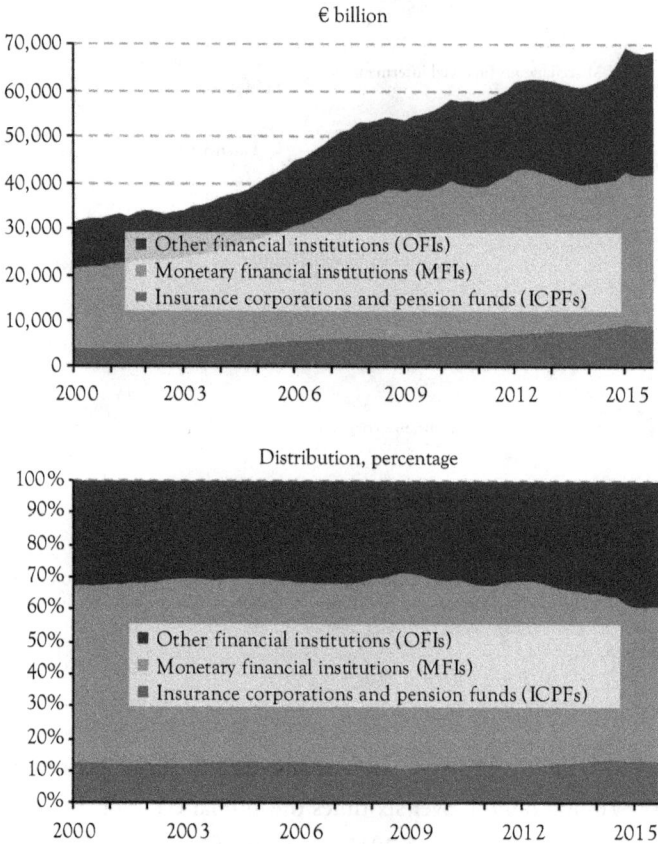

Figure 1.8 Total assets of financial intermediaries, outstanding amounts, euro area, € billion

The size of the financial sector has more than doubled since 2003. MFIs represent about half of the financing sector, but they have lost relative importance mainly due to a significant expansion of OFIs.

Source: ECB, Eurostat, and own calculations.

system as a whole, and therefore the risk embedded in it, does not seem to have declined, rather the contrary.

The size of the financial sector varies widely across countries, both in absolute and in relative terms. In absolute terms, the UK has the largest financial sector (26 percent of the total); in Germany and France, the financial sector is about half the size of that of the UK. Despite its small size of Luxembourg in terms of GDP, its financial sector is the fourth largest in the EU because of the country's role as a financial center. It is remarkable to note that the Dutch financial sector is larger than that of Italy or Spain, even though the country is between two to three times smaller. This is explained, to a certain extent, by the significant development of pension funds (Figure 1.9).

In relative terms, the countries with the largest financial systems are Luxembourg, Malta, and Ireland (with a size representing more than 20 times their respective GDP), followed by Cyprus, the Netherlands, the UK, and Denmark. On the other hand, in most eastern European countries, the financial sector represents no more than three times GDP. As discussed previously, the financial sector contributes to the efficient allocation of resources in the economy; however, excessive debt can also entail risks. Although there is no magic number indicating the optimal level of the financial sector as it depends on multiple factors, it needs to be monitored to avoid becoming excessive.[28]

In terms of composition, in most countries, MFIs account for more than half of the financial sector. The exceptions are Luxembourg, the Netherlands, Cyprus, and Malta, where OFIs are the largest sector. In the UK, Germany, Belgium, and Hungary, OFIs are also significant. ICPFs tend to be smaller across the board.

Direct Financing Through Debt and Equity Capital Markets

Besides financial intermediation, funds can also be directly channeled from savers/investors to borrowers. This may require the intervention of a financial institution to provide the infrastructure—for instance, the stock exchange—or some services—such as brokering. There are various such direct financing channels: organized markets for shares or bonds, trade credit and advances, company loans, loans from family and friends, amongst others (Figure 1.10).

Financial markets enable the pooling of resources from numerous investors. As bonds and (quoted) shares are standardized products, secondary markets can grow, enabling investors to convert their securities into liquidity at any time.

---

[28] Chapter 8 discusses the EU surveillance framework.

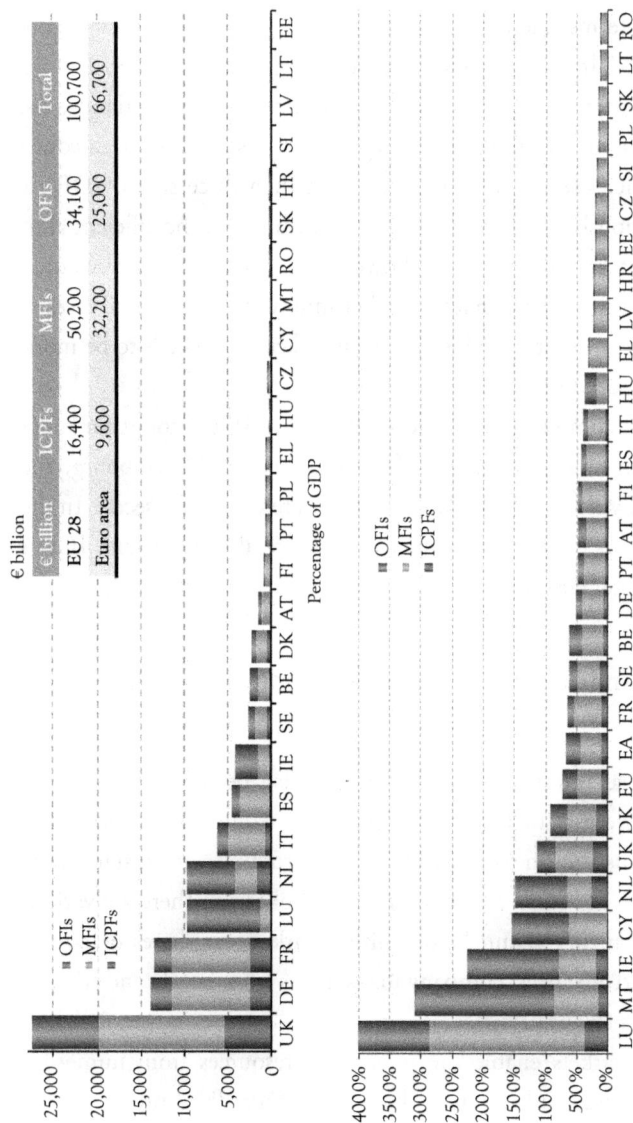

€ billion

€ billion	ICPFs	MFIs	OFIs	Total
EU 28	16,400	50,200	34,100	100,700
Euro area	9,600	32,200	25,000	66,700

Figure 1.9 Size and composition of the financial sector, total assets, 2015 € billion

The size of the financial sector varies widely across countries. In absolute terms, the United Kingdom, Germany, and France concentrate the largest share of financial institutions; in relative terms, Luxembourg, Malta, Ireland, and Cyprus are important financial centers. OFIs tend to concentrate in the largest countries or in the financial centers.

Source: ECB, Office for National Statistics (UK), Eurostat, and own calculations.

Notes: Luxembourg: OFIs = 19,000 percent of GDP. Data for Bulgaria are not available.

Providers of funds (Assets)	Direct financing through markets		Users of funds (Liabilities)
	PP		
Real economy	Bonds	Shares	Real economy
Households *NFC* *government*	CF	Advces & other	*Households* *NFC* *government*
	Equity Loans		
	PE	ABF	
Rest of the World	Direct financing outside markets		Rest of the World

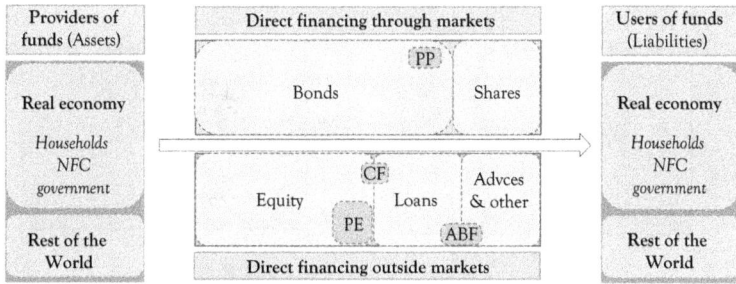

Figure 1.10 Direct financing of the economy

A variety of options are available for the real economy to obtain direct financing without the intervention of an intermediary.

Source: Own elaboration.

Notes: PP: Private placement. CF: Crowdfunding. PE: Private equity. ABF: Asset-based finance. Advces & other: Advances and other financing (includes items such as trade credit, advances by different stakeholders, tax claims and similar items). The surface of each box is proportional to the size of the sector in the euro area in 2015 (except for PP and CF, which have a very small size).

A market authority ensures the issuers seeking finance comply with a series of requirements, such as regularly disclosing information about their financial situation. The European supervisory authority in charge of ensuring the integrity, transparency, efficiency, and orderly functioning of securities markets, as well as investor protection is the European Securities Market Authority (ESMA). It works very closely with the national competent authorities, which are members of the Board of Supervisors, its highest decision-making body.[29]

In addition to a market authority, this type of direct financing requires a market infrastructure and financial institutions to provide services such as investment advice, market-making, and brokering. This can sometimes be offered by credit institutions or by independent institutions, classified under "miscellaneous financial institutions" (Figure 1.7).

While capital markets have existed for centuries, they grew rapidly in the 18th and 19th centuries during the industrial revolutions, when large amounts of money were needed to finance infrastructure—mainly railroads and canals—and the construction of large factories. In the last 30 years, markets have been boosted by three factors: (1) electronic trading, (2) technological developments, and (3) deregulation and harmonization

---

[29] For further details, see Section 7.1 and www.esma.europa.eu.

Euro area totals

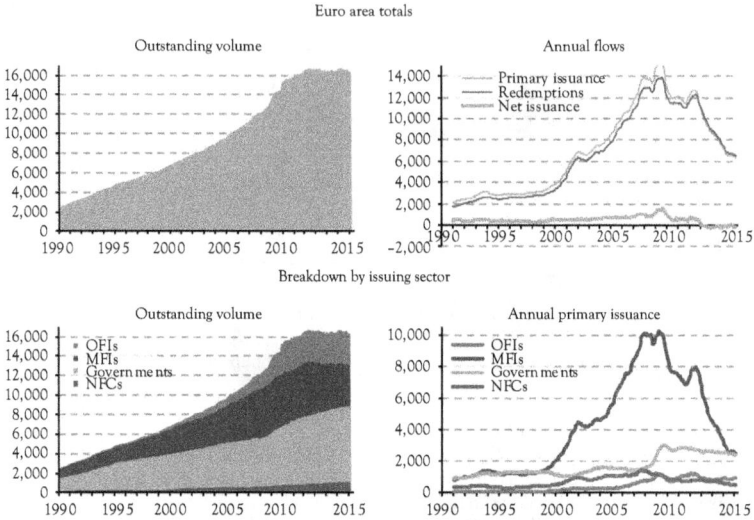

Figure 1.11 Bond markets, euro area, € billion

The volume of bonds significantly expanded until the early 2000s, when it stagnated. Bonds are mainly issued by government and MFIs. Gross flows (primary issuances and redemptions) are significantly larger than net flows, particularly for MFIs. However, they have dropped since 2009.

Source: ECB and own calculations.

Notes: Bonds issued by ICPFs are negligible (less than €60 billion of outstanding volumes) and are therefore not included.

of rules across Europe. The combination of these developments fostered a quick expansion of capital markets: between 1990 and 2008, both bond and equity markets multiplied sevenfold (Figures 1.11 and 1.14).

Bond Markets: Overview

A bond is a debt instrument, that is, the issuer has to reimburse the principal and pay interest. The need to reimburse the principal at nominal value makes bonds very different from shares in two respects. Firstly, fluctuations in bond prices are much more limited than those of shares. However, this can change when a company—or a State—is under stress and investors fear or expect a default. Secondly, bonds need to be rolled over regularly, making them somehow more liquid than shares. As a consequence, the outstanding volumes of bonds may be similar in size to annual flows—gross issuance and redemptions.

Bond markets in Europe are sizeable. They expanded steadily at an average of 9 percent a year over the period 1990–2011. Growth accelerated in the first stages of the crisis, but total volume of bonds has stagnated since early 2012 (Figure 1.11, top-left panel) at about €16,500 billion—or 160 percent of 2015 euro area GDP.

Bond markets are more or less evenly split between bonds issued by financial corporations (MFIs and OFIs, €7,400 billion) and government bonds (€7,800 billion). The volume of bonds issued by NFCs is much smaller (€1,100 billion).

Throughout the 2000s, the outstanding volume of bonds was similar in size to annual gross issuances and redemptions. This indicates that bonds had an average maturity of about one year, however, there maturities were different across sectors (Figure 1.12). The average maturity of government bonds remained between three and four years while the average maturity of bank bonds was about half a year. This is consistent with the maturity transformation function of banks and their business model based on the exploitation of the yield curve. Since the early 2000s, gross issuances were clearly dominated by MFIs—they issued over 70 percent of all euro area bonds during the peak of 2008–2010—while the outstanding volume of bonds issued by MFIs was less than 40 percent of the total. This indicates that the maturities of MFIs' bonds were much shorter than the maturities of bonds issued by other sectors.

As a response to the crisis, the ECB reduced its policy interest rates to virtually zero (Figure 4.8). This led to a significant decline not only

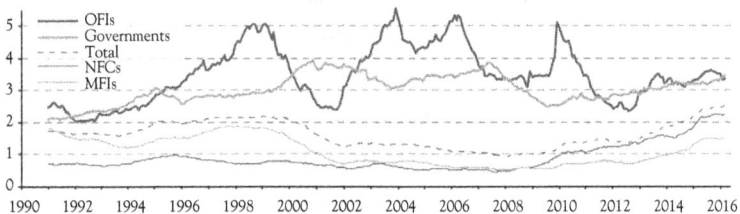

Figure 1.12 Implied maturity of bonds by issuer sector, bonds outstanding, euro area, years

The implicit maturity of bonds is different across sectors. An expansion in the maturity is observed since 2008 driven by declining (long-term) interest rates.

Source: ECB and own calculations.

Notes: The implied maturity indicates how many years are needed to redeem the total volume of bonds outstanding assuming that redemptions continue at the same rate as in the year-to-date.

of short-term interest rates but also of long-term interest rates; in other words, the yield curve declined and flattened. As a consequence, the issuance of bonds with longer maturities became more advantageous. This explains the evolution of gross issuance observed since 2010, particularly for bonds issued by MFIs (Figure 1.11, bottom-right panel). Since mid-2015, the gross issuance of bonds by MFIs has dropped to reach levels similar to the gross issuances by governments. This phenomenon is explained by a significant extension of the maturities of the bonds issued by MFIs leading to less frequent roll over needs and, therefore, less gross issuances and redemptions[30] (Figure 1.12). By mid-2015, the average implicit maturity of bonds had increased to two and a half years.

Concerns about a reduction in market liquidity in bonds markets were raised throughout 2015.[31] Although measuring liquidity involves a number of dimensions, the extension of maturities and the consequent reduction in roll over needs may explain, to a large extent, the perceived decline in market liquidity.

Bond Markets: Details by Sector

Throughout the crisis, euro area governments continuously and significantly increased the volume and flows of bonds issued: outstanding volumes expanded by more than 50 percent between 2008 and 2016 (from bout €5,000 billion to €7,800 billion) through a significant expansion in net flows. Gross issuance increased significantly in the first stages of the crisis (2008–2010) and have since remained at very high levels compared with historical series; redemptions have followed with a certain lag. After peaking in 2009, net annual issuance of bonds by governments has declined to historical averages (Figure 1.13).

This evolution in government bonds stems from the reactions to the crisis. As discussed in Chapter 2, in the early stages of the crisis, governments had to step in to support financial institutions in difficulty; such bank

---

[30] For instance, if a bond that is being rolled over every six months is substituted by a bond to be rolled over every 2 years, then gross issuances mechanically decrease by a factor of four.

[31] See, for instance, Fender and Lewrick (2015).

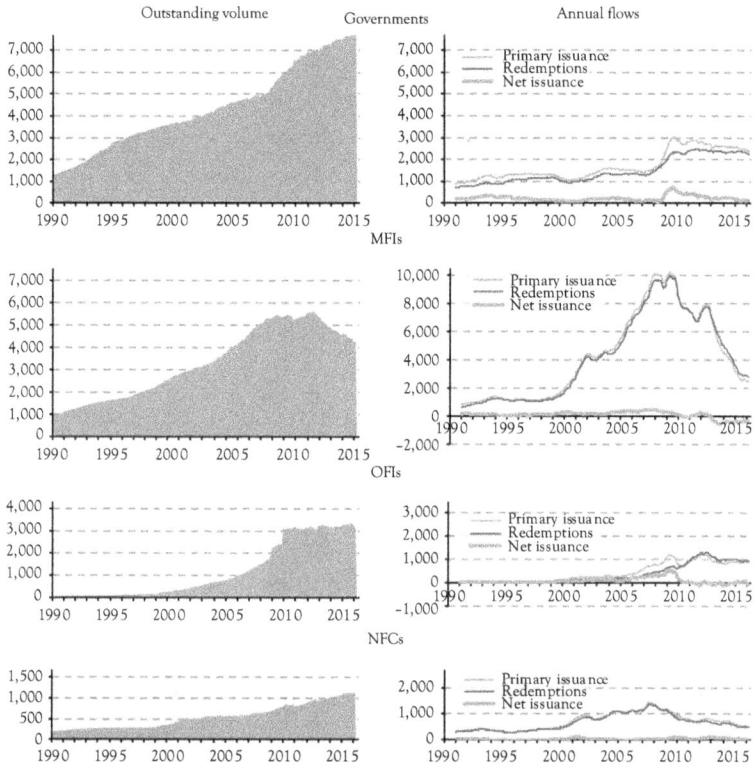

Figure 1.13 Bond issuance by sector, euro area, € billion

Beside size differences, divergent evolution is observed across sectors. The volume of bonds issued by governments and NFCs has continuously expanded while the stock of bonds issued by OFIs and MFIs have stagnated or declined since the outbreak of the crisis. Gross flows (primary issuance and redemptions) have stagnated or declined given the environment of declining interest rates.

Source: ECB and own calculations.

Notes: Bonds issued by ICPFs are negligible (less than €60 billion of outstanding volumes) and are therefore not included.

bailouts were financed by issuing debt. At the same time, economic contraction (or subdued growth) eroded public finances both on the income side (lower amounts of tax collected) and the expenditure side—higher social benefits spending linked, for instance, to unemployment—this is the so-called automatic stabilizing function of the government budget.[32] These factors have driven the expansion of the volume of government bonds.

---

[32] See also Box 1.2.

At the same time, three other drivers constrained such an expansion and explained the relative reduction in net flows and the slowdown in the growth of outstanding amounts observed from 2010 onwards. First, governments carried out a number of structural reforms to improve their finances. Second, the countries with the most acute financial problems (Greece, Ireland, Portugal and, later on, Cyprus) asked their European partners for support and discontinued or significantly reduced their issuances of new debt in the market (see Chapter 5). Finally, EU governments agreed to implement additional constraints in their public accounts by revamping economic governance rules (see Chapter 8).

To put it differently, the growth in the volume of government bonds declined from a peak of over 12 percent a year in 2009 to about 2.5 percent a year in 2015. While this implies a significant drop in growth rates, public debt continues to expand, not only in absolute terms but probably also relative to GDP (given that GDP growth is quite limited at about 2.5 percent). This reiterates the fact that leverage has not really started to decline as discussed in Section 1.2.

Bonds issued by MFIs show a totally different pattern. Their expansion, in terms of outstanding volumes, came to a halt with the outbreak of the crisis and a significant contraction occurred from late 2012, which reflects their process of deleveraging. Banks faced a number of pressures to reduce their balance sheets and leverage levels. Reducing the total size of the balance sheet implies reducing banks' assets, but also liabilities. One way of doing this is by not rolling over a (significant) share of the bonds that reach maturity.

On the other hand, a dramatic expansion in annual flows is observed between the mid-2000s and the outbreak of the crisis and a significant drop thereafter. As explained earlier, this has been driven by the rotation of the yield curve. The flat but high yield curves observed in the mid-2000s forced banks to issue bonds with very short maturities to obtain a sufficient margin from maturity transformation. With declining yields, banks may use relatively longer-term financing sources and still obtain a margin.

Bonds issued by OFIs, although initially of an order of magnitude lower than the bonds issued by governments and MFIs, significantly expanded in the run-up to the crisis. This mainly reflects the boom in securitization. The financial crisis put a halt in securitization activity (see Chapter 3). However, outstanding volumes of bonds issued by OFIs have not declined but simply stagnated since late 2009. Therefore, the contraction in securitization seems to have been offset by an equivalent expansion in the issuances of bonds by other institutions in the OFIs sector. Data on flows seem to support that interpretation: although net annual flows have fluctuated around zero, primary issuances and annual redemptions have remained at historical heights since 2010.

Finally, NFC bonds also followed a specific pattern. Although at much lower levels than any other sector, they expanded significantly both before and during the crisis. This partially reflects a certain switch from bank financing to bond financing by NFCs. Given that banks were particularly impacted by the crisis; the declining central bank rates (Figure 4.8) were translated into (declining) retail loan rates to a limited extent only and heterogeneously across countries (Figure 3.9). In this context, large corporations with investment-grade ratings could profit more from the decreasing interest rates by issuing bonds than by turning to bank credit. That being said, the slowdown in economic activity reduced the financing needs of NFCs because of its effect on demand.

Bond Markets: Specificities Across Countries

Four countries—the UK, France, Germany, and Italy—account for over 60 percent of bond issuances in the EU; this share goes up to over 75 percent when the Netherlands and Spain are included. This supposed concentration of markets stems mainly from the size of those six countries—their combined GDP also represents over 75 percent of EU GDP.

In most countries, as well as in the euro area as a whole, the government sector and the financial sector account for most bond issues (Figure 1.14). Issuance by financial institutions other than banks is particularly significant in Luxembourg, Ireland, the UK, and the Netherlands both in absolute terms and relative to their respective GDP. Luxembourg and Ireland are known to be attractive to international financial institutions as a point of entry to EU markets. By contrast, bond issuance by banks (MFIs) is particularly significant in Denmark, Sweden, and Luxembourg.

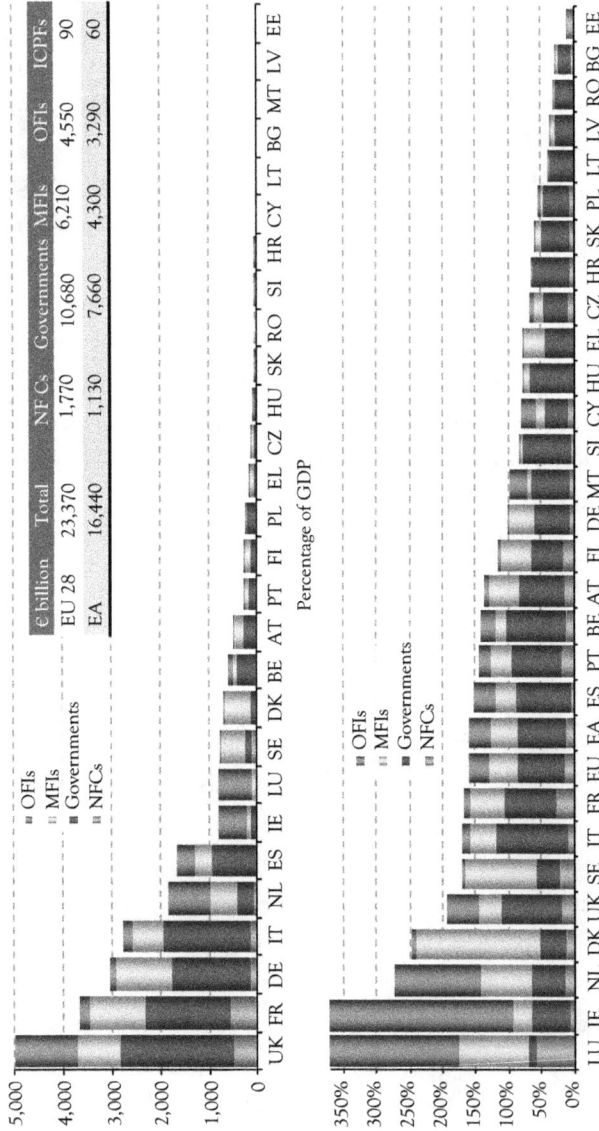

€ billion	Total	NFCs	Governments	MFIs	OFIs	ICPFs
EU 28	23,370	1,770	10,680	6,210	4,550	90
EA	16,440	1,130	7,660	4,300	3,290	60

Figure 1.14 *Issuance of bonds by country and sector, bonds outstanding, 2015*

The issuance of bonds concentrates on the largest countries (the United Kingdom, France, Germany, and Italy) although, in relative terms, they are also significant in Luxembourg, Ireland, the Netherlands, and Denmark, mainly driven by OFIs and MFIs (in the case of Denmark only).

Source: ECB and own calculations.

Notes: Luxembourg: OFIs: 1,350 percent of GDP; Ireland: OFIs: 290 percent of GDP.

With a few exceptions, bonds issued by NFCs account for about 10 percent or less of total issuance in each country and 10 percent or less of its respective GDP.

Stock Markets: Overview

Stocks have very different features from bonds. Equity instruments are, in principle, permanent, so they do not need to be rolled over. Consequently, annual issuance of equity is much smaller than the outstanding volumes and the annual issuance of bonds. Similarly, redemptions tend to be small.

Euro area equity markets (quoted shares) have a size which is less than half the size of bond markets: market capitalization hovered about €7,000 billion in 2015, or 68 percent of euro area GDP, compared with over €16,000 billion of outstanding volume of bonds. The bulk of quoted shares are issued by NFCs, while the market capitalization of banks and OFIs is much smaller (Figure 1.15, bottom-left panel). It appears that NFCs and financial corporations (MFIs and OFIs) have opposite

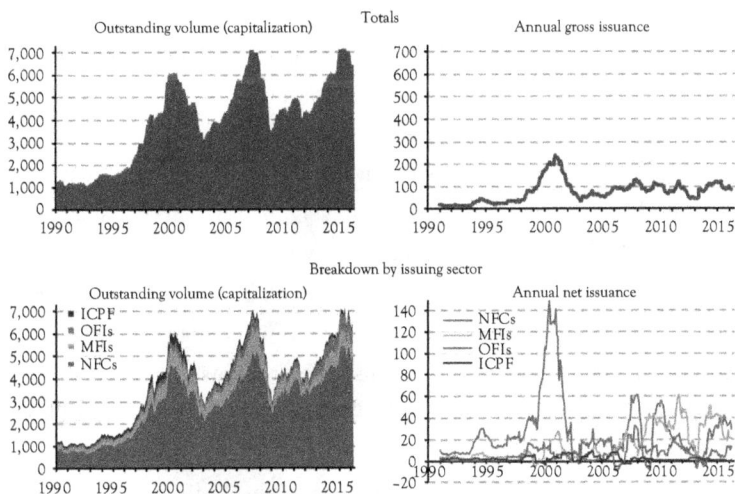

Figure 1.15 Equity markets, euro area, € billion

The volume of equity securities evolves with much more volatility than in the case of bonds. Given the permanent nature of equity, issuance is significantly smaller than capitalization. The bulk of stocks has been issued by nonfinancial corporations.

Source: ECB: securities statistics and own calculations.

preferences in their mix of quoted shares (equity) and bonds as a source of funding. NFCs make extensive use of equity markets as a source of funding and much more limited used of bond markets; while financial corporations use bond markets extensively and issue equity to a much lesser extent.

Market capitalization is significantly affected by price fluctuations, which reflect actual revenues or losses but also other factors such as the outlook of the firm, investor confidence and other psychological factors. Stock markets tend to have a more volatile evolution than bond markets and can sometimes be affected by the dynamics of bubbles (Box 1.4).

Box 1.4 Financial and Economic Bubbles

Many episodes of financial bubbles have occurred throughout history. As early as in the 17th century, the tulip mania in the Netherlands is known as one of the first bubbles. Maritime transport in the 18th century and railway construction in the 19th century also generated financial bubbles—for instance, the South Sea Company, the Mississippi Company, or the Railway Mania. In the 20th century, bubbles were mainly rooted in stock exchanges or in housing: the roaring twenties leading to the crash of 1929, the Asian financial crisis of 1997 or the dotcom bubble of 1996–2001.

The data on flows of quoted shares clearly depict the blowing up and the burst of the dotcom bubble (Figure 1.15). Net issuance of shares by NFCs—mainly firms dealing with new technologies—skyrocketed from €20 billion a year to over €140 billion a year. This went hand in hand with a widespread hype and increasing demand, which multiplied the prices of these stocks. This explains, to a large extent, the rise in capitalization from €1,500 billion to over €4,500 billion. However, at a certain point, investors realized that this was not sustainable and stopped buying new shares—the "Minsky moment."[33]

---

[33] The "Minsky moment" refers to a sudden collapse of assets values following a long period of prosperity and increasing value of investments.

The artificially high stock prices were corrected and capitalization went down to almost €2,000 billion.

The recent financial crisis that started in 2007 seems to be the outcome of a similar pattern—capitalization increased from €2,000 billion to over €5,000 billion and subsequently collapsed back to almost €2,000 billion. However, the evolution of net issuance had nothing to do with the ones observed in the late 90s. This is explained by the fact that the 2007–2008 bubble did not arise in the stock exchange but in credit and housing prices.[34] Net flows of bank loans to households and firms increased significantly throughout the early 2000s (Annex 1.1); a significant expansion in net interbank and interfinancial loans is also observed during that period. The turmoil in Chinese markets that started in summer 2015 or the Volkswagen scandal related to the gas emissions uncovered in September 2015 seemed to have had a contained impact in euro area stock markets. However, with the turn of 2016 a bear mood seems to have settled in the markets. Although past performance cannot be used to make exact predictions of future evolution of stocks, it is quite likely that the capitalization of euro area stocks will continue to correct until bottoming out at about €4,000 billion.

An important difference between the dotcom bubble and the financial bubble of 2007–2008 is the availability of capital buffers to accommodate the burst. More than half of the financing of NFCs comes from equity (Figure 1.5); therefore, they have a large buffer to absorb shocks, and losses are borne by the investors responsible of the decisions of the companies in difficulties. This allowed a quick cleanup of problematic balance sheets in the dotcom bubble without major contagion to other economic agents. The buffers available in bank balance sheets—and those of financial institutions in general—are much smaller.[35] Given this lack of buffers, the excesses cannot be corrected through prices and losses but by issuing new equity, but this

---

[34] For a more detailed analysis of the origins of the crisis, see Part B.

[35] In other words, the technological bubble was unleveraged while the 2007–2008 bubble was highly leveraged.

can take a long period of time. Indeed, since the outbreak of the crisis, the issuance of quoted shares, particularly by banks, has remained at very high levels for historical standards (Figure 1.15). Having said that, public authorities and analysts should cautiously assess if such levels of net issuance of equity are indeed used to address the weaknesses of the banks surfaced on the wake of the 2007–2008 crisis or if rather a new bubble is in the making.

The latest technological developments have led to a radical change in how markets operate and to an acceleration and amplification of economic bubbles. Indeed, electronic trading has substituted outcry auctions; retail investors do not need to interact with their bank through a physical or telephonic contact but they can just trade through Internet from home and, more recently, from anywhere with a portable device; professional investors have developed algorithms to trade at the nanosecond. All these factors have played an important role in the dotcom bubble of the early 2000s, in the one of 2007–2008, and in the more recent events in China. Moreover, advances in IT have made the financial and the real economy much more interconnected at global level.[36]

Stock Markets: Specificities Across Countries

Three countries, the UK, Germany, and France concentrate almost 60 percent of the shares issued across the EU in absolute terms (Figure 1.16, top panel). However, the largest markets relative to GDP are those of Ireland, Luxembourg, Sweden, Denmark, and the Netherlands (Figure 1.16, bottom panel). In the majority of countries, the bulk of quoted shares are issued by NFCs. However, in a few countries—Malta, Luxembourg, the Netherlands, and Bulgaria—OFIs issued more than 30 percent of all shares in terms of capitalization and, in a few others— Slovakia, Poland, Malta, Hungary, Czech Republic, and Greece—shares issued by MFIs are also relatively significant—representing about 30 percent or more of all quoted shares.

---

[36] For further details about bubbles, see Brunnermeier and Schnabel (2015), Jorda, Schularickand, and Taylor (2015) or Reinhart and Rogoff (2011).

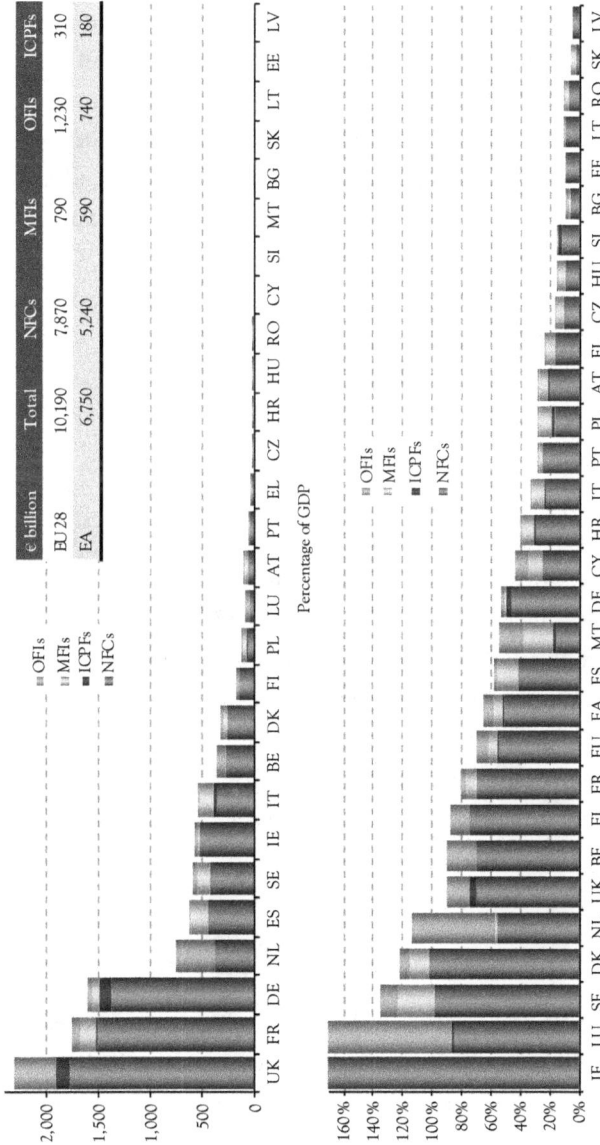

€ billion	Total	NFCs	MFIs	OFIs	ICPFs
EU28	10,190	7,870	790	1,230	310
EA	6,750	5,240	590	740	180

Figure 1.16 Issuance of quoted shares by country and sector, capitalization outstanding, 2015

The bulk of EU stock markets concentrate in the United Kingdom, France, and Germany, although stock markets are also significant in Ireland, Luxembourg, Sweden, Denmark, and the Netherlands, relative to their respective GDP. NFCs represent the lion share of equity securities, with the exception of Luxembourg and the Netherlands, where the stocks issued by OFIs have a similar size to NFCs stocks.

Source: ECB and own calculations.

Notes: Luxembourg: OFIs = 90 percent of GDP. Shares issued in Luxembourg by MFIs are nil; this indicates that (listed) banks with subsidiaries in Luxembourg issue their shares in their country of origin. Ireland: NFCs: 240 percent of GDP; MFIs = 15 percent of GDP; OFIs = 10 percent of GDP; ICPFs = 0 percent.

Direct Financing Beyond Capital Markets

Besides investors and financial intermediaries, a number of other stake-holders are critical to the day-to-day life of businesses and to economic production in general: employees, customers, suppliers, public authorities, services providers, educational systems, and so on. Economic transactions between suppliers and clients, and between companies and employees, imply intrinsic financing resources that can be provided neither by capital markets nor by the financial sector. These sources of funding arise from the difference between the continuous accrual of economic value and the point-in-time nature of payments and settlement. While they are mostly short-term, they are still critical for a well-functioning economy. Wages, trade credit, utilities and tax claims are common examples. Although they entail direct financing between two economic agents, the financial sector can still play a role by providing some services linked to these bilateral positions—such as asset-based lending, factoring, and leasing.

Nonetheless, these "alternative" sources of funding may also have a long-term nature. This can be the case for intercompany loans, government subsidies, internal funding, or equity provided by family and friends. While there is much less data and information about all these sources of information, they represent the bulk of the financing of the real economy. For instance, about one third of the financing of NFCs takes the form of equity other than quoted shares (see Figure 1.5), which corresponds to the initial contributions needed to start a family business and the subsequent profits ploughed back into the firm.

Beyond the Static Structure of Funding

Up until this point, we have mainly described the funding structure of the economy for the different agents individually. However, individuals and firms are not isolated; the interactions between different actors determine, to a large extent, how individual positions evolve over time. Therefore, this section discusses more in detail the interconnectedness among all market participants and what this implies in moments of financial stress such as during the recent financial crisis.

Interconnectedness and Contagion

Banks play a central role in the financial system: insurance corporations form groups with banks through "bank/insurance" holding companies; insurance corporations, pension funds and investment funds provide financing to MFIs by buying their securities; financial vehicle corporations channel the securitization activities of various financial intermediaries (mainly banks), which nevertheless may retain a significant chunk of an issuance; and many of the companies classified as "miscellaneous financial institutions" are in fact subsidiaries of credit institutions. Moreover, banks are connected with each other through interbank lending markets (Figure 1.17).

Banks and financial institutions are not only interconnected with each other but they are also closely interlinked with the real economy. Through their intermediation function, financial institutions obtain financial resources from some households and NFCs and provide credit to other households and NFCs, as well as to governments. Moreover, firms are closely interconnected with a large number of stakeholders, including suppliers, customers, employees, and civil society.

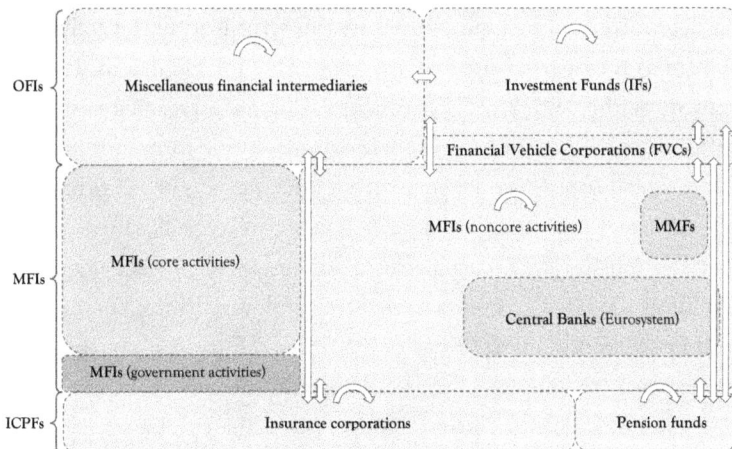

Figure 1.17 Interconnections within the financial sector: positions

The various components of the financial sector interact with each other creating a highly connected network.

Source: Own elaboration.

Notes: The surface of each box is proportional to the size of the sector in the euro area in 2015.

As shown in Section 1.1, the interconnection among the various parts of the economy can lead to feedback loops where the weaknesses or the strengths of a sector impacts other sectors with potentially amplified effects. For instance, a government in financial difficulties may pay suppliers late; some of these suppliers may be confronted with cash constraints and therefore pay salaries late; employees paid late will probably need to postpone some of their spending and therefore consumption will weaken; consequently, retailers will reduce their orders and factories will reduce their production with both potentially reducing their labor force; this will further exacerbate the difficulties for paying suppliers and employees and further decrease consumption.

While the economy is formed of a complex network of financial interconnections, not all of these interconnections have the same features.[37] In particular, the bond between two economic agents can be very closely tied or very loose. This is crucial to understanding how the crisis unfolded (Part B) and the political response vis-à-vis the financial sector (Parts C and D) and the real economy (Part E). Depending on the distance in the relationship between two economic agents, their fate may be more or less dependent on each other.

In this context, a first distinction appears between equity instruments and debt instruments. Equity investors can scrutinize all the activities of the firm as they participate and are responsible for the day-to-day management of the company. Consequently, they take great interest in the performance of the company as their rewards, in the form of returns, are closely linked to the income generated by the business of the firm.

Employees and firms are usually bonded by very close ties, a long-term relationship and mutual trust. For instance, in many countries, large firms are legally required to involve employees (through representatives) in the important decisions of the firm. Staff interest may be closely aligned with the interest of shareholders and the firm. Furthermore, in companies that take the form of cooperatives, the employees are in fact

---

[37] A detailed overview of the so-called network analysis goes beyond the scope of this book. Interested readers can consult, for instance, Castrén and Rancan (2013); Hautony and Héamz (2014); Haldane (2015).

the shareholders. Given this framework, whenever a firm is in difficulty, employees may accept some sacrifices—such as a delay in the payment of wages for a couple of months or a reduction in the salary—in the hope of contributing to the survival of the firm and, therefore, to that of their own jobs.

The relationship between a firm and its long-term suppliers and customers has similar features. Most suppliers search for long-term commercial relationships rather than a specific order, therefore a supplier may accept to be paid later than initially agreed if a customer is facing temporary difficulties.

Other stakeholders provide funding to the company in the form of bank loans or through the purchase of bonds in the market. This type of investor is interested in the company's performance insofar as it ensures their investment is repaid with the agreed interest. They maintain an arm's length relationship without participating in the management of the firm and without an insider's view of the company—although this is partially mitigated by greater transparency requirements for companies issuing in the markets or by the documentation required by the bank before granting a loan.

The proximity of the ties translates into the debt ranking or degree of "subordination" of the different stakeholders of a firm. Salaries and trade credit are, in general, subordinated to bank loans and bonds are more "senior." While, in principle, such a debt ranking has legal implications for an insolvent firm being liquidated ("gone concern"); in fact, the ranking already has an effect in the normal life of the firm ("going concern").[38] Indeed, a company have high incentives to pay its bonds on time and avoid a downgrade of the rating, what could lead the firm to be excluded from the market. However, the very same company has much more leeway to stretch the payments to suppliers and employees, which are therefore more junior.

---

[38] Note that the effective degree of subordination for a going concern firm may differ from the legal subordination order in a liquidation context.

Impact of The Crisis

"Distance" investors tend to retrieve their funding with the first sings of financial turmoil while junior stakeholders tend to be engaged for longer with the companies during difficult times. For instance, many of the investors in large quoted companies can be considered as distance investors; their fund withdrawals are behind the collapse in stock markets observed in 2008 and 2009 (see Figure 1.15). Similarly, the collapse of noncore assets and liabilities of banks illustrates how quickly senior investors can withdraw their positions in moments of turmoil (Figure 1.18).[39] On the other hand, junior stakeholders would strive to support the firm, due to their close ties and their lower mobility. As a consequence, the effects of the crisis on junior stakeholders are smoother but may last much longer.

Data on sales illustrate how a slow doom loop has resulted in deteriorating economic activity. Moreover, they also reflect the severity of the recent crisis compared to previous crises. For instance, car registrations fell by 25 percent from peak to trough, three times more than in the aftermath of the dotcom crisis, when they fell by 8 percent (Figure 1.19) and for a much longer period than in the early 2000s or the mid-1990s. Similarly, spending on basic articles such as food and clothing fell continuously from a peak in the mid-2000s all the way through 2014 (Figure 1.20).

These data should be interpreted against the implications for junior stakeholders. For instance, the local butcher may be making some sacrifices to keep the business working instead of closing down the business. However, stretching the financial capacity of junior stakeholders can have a marked negative feedback effect by reducing aggregate demand and triggering a vicious circle. A potential solution for the difficulties of an isolated company—for instance, the local butcher—may have devastating consequences at macroeconomic level if this is generalized—this is the so-called paradox of thrift. Moreover, car and retail sales are just an

---

[39] Chart 1.18 also illustrates the interconnection and central position of banks vis-à-vis the financial sector (noncore assets and liabilities) and vis-à-vis the real economy (core assets and liabilities) and how banks constitute the connecting link between the financial sector and the real economy.

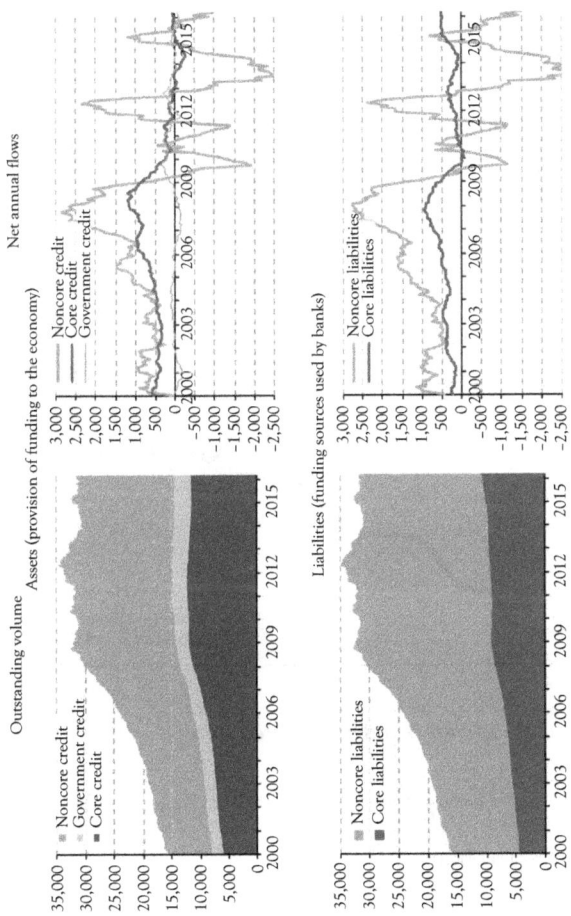

Figure 1.18 Core versus noncore activities of banks, euro area MFIs, € billion

Noncore activities (credit and liabilities) have outgrowth core activities. Noncore activities present a high volatility and seem to be closely Interconnected with the outbreak and subsequent stages of the crisis.

Source: ECB and own calculations.

Notes: Core credit: credit provided by banks to households and NFCs through loans or the purchase of securities. Government credit: loans to governments and holdings of sovereign bonds. Noncore credit is calculated as the residual factor with respect to total assets. M3 is used as a proxy for core liabilities. Noncore liabilities are calculated as the difference between total assets and M3. Government liabilities are negligible and, therefore, are not shown. Annual flows are computed as the sum of net flows for 12 consecutive months through a rolling window. "Net" refers to new transactions minus redemptions.

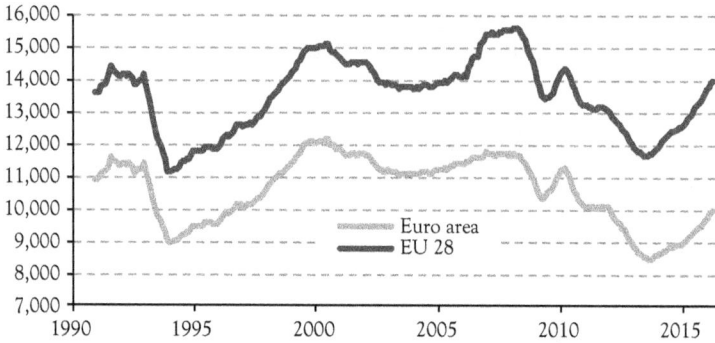

Figure 1.19 *Car registrations, passenger cars, number of cars (thousands), year-to-date sum*

Car registrations–given that cars are long term and high value assets–provide an indication of the impact of the crisis on the real economy.

Source: ECB, Eurostat, and own calculations.

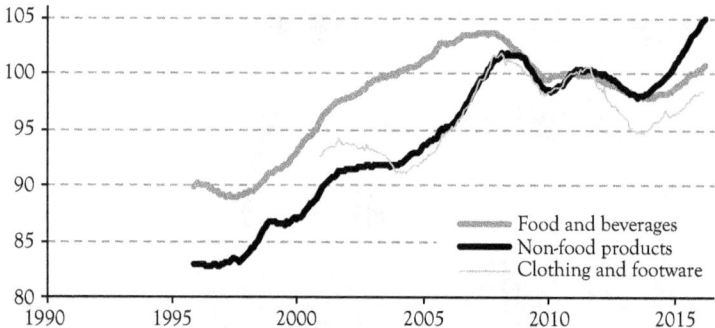

Figure 1.20 *Retail sales, turnover index, deflated, one-year moving average*

Retail sales of basic need items provide an indication of how the recent crisis was significantly more serious than previous recessions.

Source: ECB, Eurostat, and own calculations.

indication of the broader situation in the economy, given the direct contacts with all kind of services and industrial production.

The crisis also affected the junior stakeholder of governments, such as suppliers or public employees. Many governments were under such financial stress in Europe so as to warrant their application for support from their European partners.[40] Other countries, confronted with increasing debt costs (Figure 2.5), also embarked in austerity measures. Although no government defaulted on their bonds during the crisis,[41] they did stretch payments on other instruments. The junior character of wages appears clearly in the fact that salaries were frozen or reduced in countries like Greece, Portugal, or Spain.[42] Suppliers were also significantly stretched. For instance, late payments had reached such a magnitude in Spain that the central government had to create a fund to support the liquidity of local and regional governments.[43] But this was not an isolated case, many other countries were in a similar situation. In other words, public employees and suppliers have contributed to—or have borne the cost of—alleviating the burden of public finances in many Member States.

Similarly, data indicate that many bank borrowers were unable to repay their debts and nonperforming loans skyrocketed in many countries (Figure 3.4).[44] Given that bank loans or mortgages are the last thing that one stops paying, a company or a household that has defaulted on a bank loan has also stretched payments with respect to other (more junior) debtors. Therefore, the financial strain in employees or suppliers can be assumed to be at least as high as that which is implicit in the trend on nonperforming loans.

The economic slowdown eventually translated into increasing unemployment figures (Figure 1.21), which also provide an indication of the potential decline in aggregate demand. Given that in many cases companies had postponed payment of wages for months before eventually filing for bankruptcy, the actual impact on spending or aggregate demand was larger than what may be deduced from the evolution of

---

[40] See Chapter 5.

[41] In the case of Greece, there was a restructuring of public debt to relieve the burden on public accounts, but this was officially a voluntary exchange of debt, not a default (see Box 5.2).

[42] In some cases, the reductions in salaries were declared void by constitutional courts. See, for instance, Hope and Atkins (2014); Papadimas (2014); Khalip and Gonçalves (2013).

[43] This was implemented through the Royal Decree Law 7/2012.

[44] As a general rule, loans are classified as nonperforming if they are over 90 days past their due date.

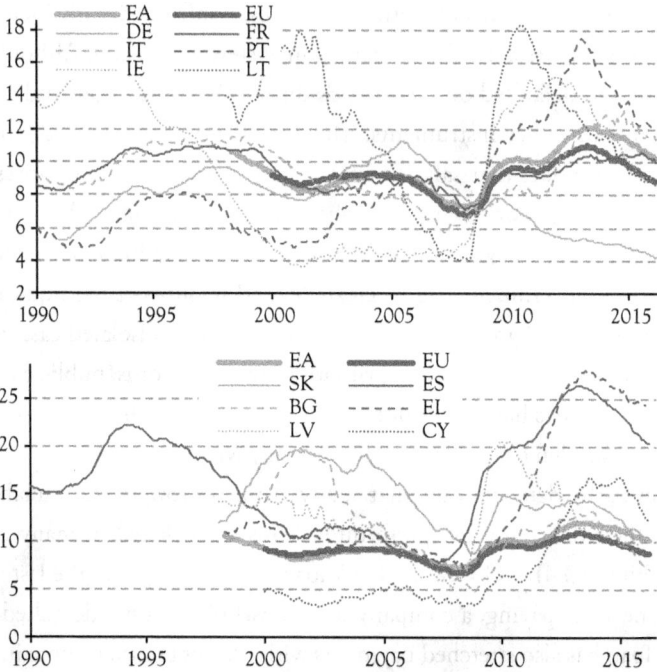

Figure 1.21 Unemployment rate, euro area, European Union, and selected countries, seasonally adjusted series

Countries have different cycles and different unemployment levels. However, all of them have been significantly impacted by the recent crisis. And improvement is observed across the board since 2013, but unemployment rates remain quite high in most countries.

Source: ECB, Eurostat, and own presentation.

unemployment figures. Moreover, people's general economic "mood" and their expectations about the future translate into demand for goods and services. Ordinary citizens who feel the outlook for them and their families is bright are more likely to embark on economic projects. When the outlook is gloomy, they will be more cautious with their spending. It is generally accepted that the value of financial assets, such as quoted shares, reflect expectations about the future. A similar logic applies to households and their spending behavior and thus current GDP.[45]

---

[45] The negative mood turned into a malaise broader than just economic, as reflected in the general rise of populist and extremist parties.

Coming back to car sales, they provide not only an indication of the current situation, but also an indication about expectations for the future. Cars are long-term assets and need to be replaced after a few years. But when times are hard, replacement can be postponed. Moreover, because cars are usually purchased against a loan, trends in car sales provide information about the assessment of the current economic situation and the economic outlook, by both credit institutions and prospective buyers.

Although there is some leeway for stretching one component or the another of an economic system, an appropriate balance between all components is essential for the system to function smoothly. Households and junior stakeholders are the foundation of the financial economy as they are the ultimate providers of funding. Despite the sacrifices reflected in the evolution of unemployment rates and retails sales, households continued to provide funding to the economy. Although they have significantly declined, net flows of core liabilities of banks—deposits of households and NFCs—remained positive (Figure 1.18). In other words, contrary to senior investors, households and NFCs did not fly away with their funding. However, as long as households are unable to properly generate resources and savings, even the most advanced financial sector cannot intermediate or efficiently channel funding to projects in need of investment.

The pivotal role of households as ultimate providers of funding and the importance of demand should not be underestimated. It seems that financial stability and economic prosperity will only be restored when junior creditors get relieved from their situation of financial stress. Besides indicating the activity of retailers, data on sales can also be read from the perspective of consumers. In this context, data point not only to a significant deterioration on aggregate demand but also in living conditions given that the expenditure in basic items such as food, beverage and clothing have declined by more than 10 percent. Indeed, it has been argued that an important driver behind the dynamics explained in this section is the phenomenon of increasing inequality paired with over indebtedness and debt overhang.[46]

---

[46] For further details, see Annex 2.1.

Conclusion

This introductory chapter provides an overview of the circulation of funds within an economy through the different financing channels. While bilateral interactions between economic agents generate the bulk of the financial positions, the financial sector plays an important role in mobilizing additional resources. All these financial positions imply a complex network of interconnections. Weaknesses and strengths can quickly spread throughout the network in vicious or virtuous circles. The financial crisis triggered one such vicious circle (see Part B for further details).

It also discusses how senior stakeholders, such as capital investors, can be highly mobile and how some of them rush out at initial signs of turmoil.[47] This quick withdrawal of funds affected firstly the financial sector and governments and, therefore, one of the first reactions to the crisis was to support them (Part C). Once the situation was stabilized, governments embarked in a process of fixing the flaws in order to attract investors back to Europe (Part D and Chapter 9). Improving financial conditions in financial markets—such as lower yields—and positive macroeconomic indicators—such as GDP growth—are usually considered preconditions for a robust recovery.

The financial sector plays a central role in supporting the productive system to generate value and welfare for citizens. However, policies addressing exclusively the financial sector are not sufficient to put the European economy back to a growth path. Therefore, public authorities have also implemented a series of measures aiming at reactivating demand (Chapter 9).

Annex 1.1 Dynamics in the Circulation of Funds

The main text provides an overview of the financial positions of the different institutional sectors. These stocks indicate the financial exposures

---

[47] Many authors explain how the recent financial crisis has been linked to the erosion of confidence in wholesale markets. See, for instance, Cœuré (2013); Krugman (2013); Gorton and Metrick (2012); Varoufakis (2011); Abbassi and Schnabel (2009) or Cochrane (2014). See also Chapter 3.

between agents that have been built up over the years. However, they offer limited information about recent dynamics. In order to complement the static view of stocks, this annex provides a brief overview of the type of information stemming from flows, that is, the new assets and liabilities incurred during a given period. Although flows are therefore closely connected with the stocks, the use of flows provides a totally different perspective.

Total Assets and Liabilities

The evolution of net flows of assets and net flows of liabilities and the difference between both[48] provides an indication of the funding capacity generated or absorbed by a given sector (Figure A.1). Flows are an order of magnitude smaller than volumes (Figures 1.3 and 1.4). For instance, the volume of assets and liabilities for households were €22,000 billion and €7,000 billion, respectively, while flows hovered about €500 billion in the early 2000s and even much below more recently. This is explained by the fact that the stocks of assets and liabilities are the result of the accumulation of flows over a long period of time.

As a consequence, stocks are embedded with high levels of inertia and can conceal the impact of the crisis in the different sectors, which appears clearly in the series of flows. Flows for NFCs follow the economic cycle very closely,[49] although with a short lag. Indeed, after the dotcom bubble of the early 2000s, net transactions of NFCs' assets and liabilities tracked the expansion of the mid 2000s, the burst of the bubble in the late 2000s, the short recovery of 2009–2010 and the second dip of 2012, and the incipient recovery starting in late 2014.

---

[48] Flows or transactions are expressed in net terms, that is, actual new assets (or liabilities) minus redemption of assets (or liabilities) over the period. It should not be confused with "net" as in net financial worth, which refers to assets minus liabilities in a given moment in time. Note that the change in the balance sheet depends not only on transactions but also on valuation changes—for instance, as a result of foreign exchange fluctuations—and other changes.

[49] GDP growth (Box 9.1) can be used as a proxy for the economic cycle.

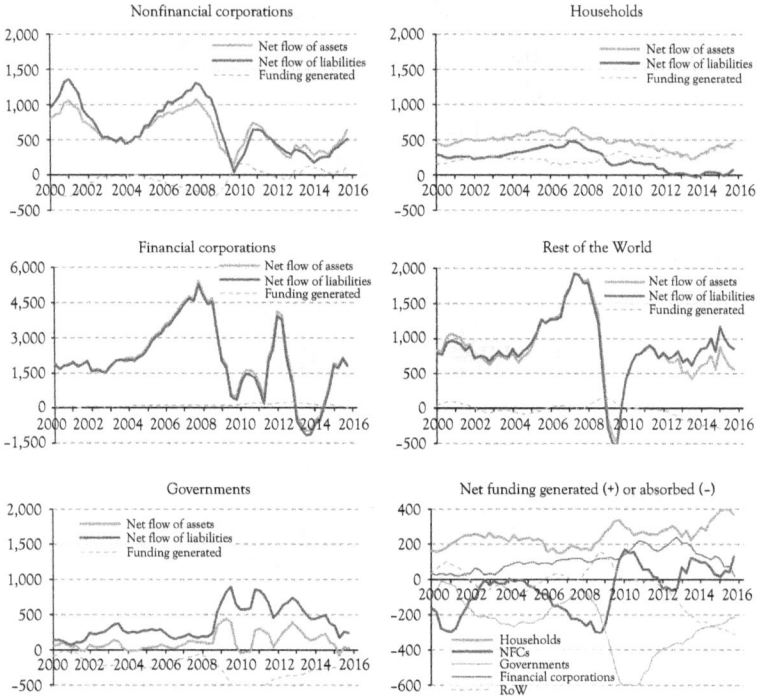

Figure A.1 *Dynamics in assets (funding generation) and liabilities (funding absorption), net annual flows, euro area, € billion*

Real transactions generate financial assets and liabilities. The various panels show the impact of the crisis across the five institutional sectors of the euro area.

Source: ECB, Eurostat, and own elaboration.

Note: The scale for financial corporations is three times larger than for the other sectors. The funding capacity generated corresponds to the difference between net flows of assets and net flows of liabilities; when it is negative it indicates a net absorption of funding by that sector.

NFCs' financial liabilities are larger than financial assets (Figures 1.3 and 1.4). Similarly, net flow of liabilities was traditionally larger than the net flow of assets, in other words, NFCs were receiving financing from other sectors to fund their tangible assets such as buildings, machinery, and stocks. However, the situation has reversed since the outbreak of the crisis with NFCs becoming net providers of funding for other sectors. This is mainly explained by four driving forces closely intertwined with the slowdown in economic activity: a decline in the demand, an excess of capacity leading to the disposal of some tangible assets, difficulties for obtaining new credit, and the process of reducing the debtor position and deleverage. Despite the starting of the economic recovery in 2015, most of those four processes seem to continue given that the flow of liabilities remains below the flow of assets.

As for stocks, households are the main generators of funding for the rest of the economy in terms of flows. Indeed, throughout the crisis, the capacity of households to fund the rest of the economy has been an important cushion to avoid an even bigger downturn. Households in the need of funding had difficulties to access credit as reflected in the significant decline in net flows of liabilities to zero or even negative values. However, other households kept significant levels of savings—as reflected in positive net flows of assets—which become sources of funding for other sectors. On balance, households have provided increasing amounts of funding to the rest of the economy since the outbreak of the crisis.

While a proper balance between the various institutional sectors of the economy is important, at the end of the day, households are the most important sector as it consists of the citizens. Therefore, the drivers of net flows of households' assets and liabilities deserved a more thorough reflection. It is quite possible that the dynamics of households' assets and liabilities may be linked to the increasing concentration of income in the highest quantiles. It is widely acknowledged that high income individuals tend to save more than lower income individuals, who use most of their income for consumption.[50] Therefore, the very low net transactions observed for households' liabilities throughout the crisis may be explained, to a large extent, by the high levels of unemployment (see Section 1.7) and the difficulties to obtain credit by large parts of the population. This is also reflected in the increasing level of nonperforming loans (Figure 3.4). It has been argued that the increasing level of inequality can negatively affect economic growth[51] and can be a factor explaining the difficulties of the European economy to resolutely take off and leave the crisis behind.

---

[50] The so-called wealth effects have also an important impact on inequality. The price of financial assets increased often even in bad times, but this benefitted only the wealthy households.

[51] See Annex 2.1.

Net flows of financial intermediaries' assets and liabilities are three times larger than net flows for NFCs or households. Moreover, they present quick and large swings.[52] These high levels of volatility can have important consequences for stability, not only within the financial sector, but also for the larger economy. For instance, the contagion of financial distress from the banking sector to the public sector has widely been acknowledged.[53] Similarly, contagion to solvent households and NFCs in the form of a credit crunch cannot be discarded. Finally, the analysis of flows confirms that the financial sector does not generate funding but simply intermediate between agents. Indeed, in a moment where the flow of assets and liabilities of financial corporations was over €5,000 billion—and their balance sheet over €50,000 billion—the financial sector was not even able to generate €150 billion of fresh new funding for other sectors.

The movements in governments' flows are explained, to a large extent, by the significant amounts of capital injected by public authorities in the early stages of the crisis to support the financial sector.[54] On top of that, the series on governments reflect the automatic stabilizers (see Box 1.2). Those two phenomena explain the significant increases in the net financing needs or deficit of the public sector in the initial phases of the crisis. The contraction in the net financing needs observed since 2010 is explained by the improvement in the economic outlook, but also by the more stringent economic governance rules.[55]

The collapse in the flows of the external sector observed in 2008–2009 stems from the repatriation of funds by foreigners investing in the euro area and the repatriation of funds by euro area residents investing abroad. This is explained by the low attachment of foreign investors to their financial investments and the high mobility of capital (see Section 1.7). A decoupling in the evolution of assets and liabilities is observed since late 2011 leading to a continuous deterioration in the international net financial position of the euro area.

---

[52] Given their size, MFIs' drive the profile of the overall financial sector.

[53] See Chapter 3.

[54] See Chapters 3 and 4.

[55] See Chapter 8.

The impact of the crisis on the behavior of the different sectors is summarized in the series on net funding generated or absorbed (Figure A.1 bottom-right panel). Households, as a whole, have provided financing to the rest of the economy throughout the whole crisis period. The financial sector has also supported the rest of the economy, although less and less so since 2012—and this is achieved through significant levels of leverage. NFCs have become net providers of funding to the rest of the economy. Governments have activated their shock absorption function by increasing their indebtedness and making nonrefundable transfers to other sectors in the economy. Finally, net repatriation of funds by the external sectors has significantly increased since 2012, signaling negative developments either in the competitiveness of the euro area economy or in the international confidence about the euro area. However, turmoil in other parts of the world—China, Brazil, and other countries—may also be playing a role in the international movements of capital.

Nonfinancial Corporations: Breakdown by Instrument

As an example of the information provided by flows, we present hereafter an overview of the role of the different components of NFCs' assets (Figure A.2) and liabilities (Figure A.3). NFCs seem to hold bonds as a safe investment in moments of financial turmoil; probably mainly sovereign bonds of strong economies. However, investment fund shares seem to be used for obtaining returns for excess liquidity or idle resources. Indeed, with the intensification of the financial turmoil in 2008, a flight to security from investment funds to bonds is observed. Thereafter, NFCs seem to have divested their holdings—assets—in both investment funds and bonds to obtain funding and liquidity.

In the period 2004–2007, data show an increasing accumulation of currency and deposits, probably beyond transactional needs. A temporary placement of this excess cash on liquid assets may explain the increasing purchase of quoted shares observed between 2006 and 2008 and the subsequent decline when the inflows of currency and deposits decreased.

The series on "other assets" is composed mainly of trade credit and advances provided, which are both closely linked to the turnover of the company and, therefore, the economic cycle. This series also provides an

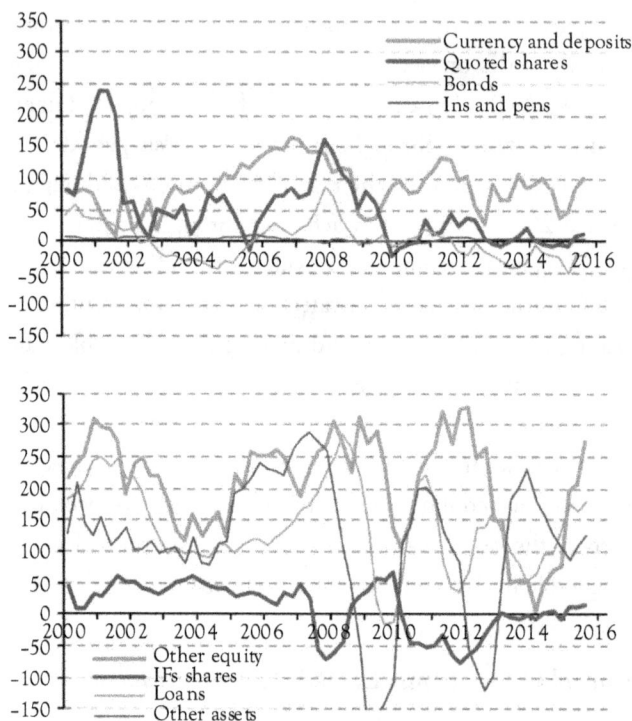

Figure A.2 Dynamics in NFCs' financial assets, net annual flows, euro area, € billion

In general, NFCs have continued to increase their assets throughout the crisis, although with high volatility. This means that they have been a source of fresh new funding for other sectors. NFCs provide resources mainly in the form of nonquoted equity, other assets–mainly trade credit–and loans.

Source: ECB, Eurostat, and own calculations.

Notes: "Ins and pens": insurance, pension and standardized guarantee schemes.

indication of the extent of the boom in the second half of the 2000s and of the impact of the subsequent recession. Subsequently, the series track the short recovery of 2010, the second dip of 2012, and the incipient recovery starting in 2015.

The accumulation of cash buffers—currency and deposits—during the boom may have also driven the expansion in the loans granted by firms to other economic agents—payment facilities for customers or intragroup loans. This may have been offered as an alternative to trade credit and is consistent with the shift from bank loans to other loans

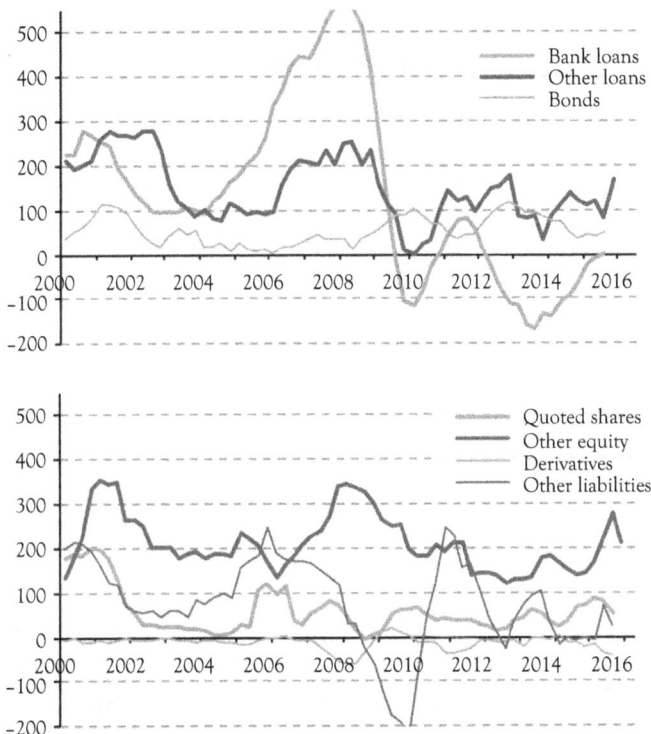

Figure A.3 Dynamics in NFCs' liabilities, net annual flows, euro area, € billion

The crisis had a large impact on the access of NFCs to bank loans: aggregate reimbursements in the economy outgrew new loans and net annual flows became negative. The recourse to other liabilities–mainly trade credit–was also significantly affected.

Source: ECB, Eurostat, and own calculations.

observed in households' liabilities[56] and with the increase in net flows of other loans on the liabilities side of NFCs' balance sheets (Figure A.3). The provision of payment facilities by NFCs has gotten renewed traction since early 2014.

Equity other than quoted shares clearly stands out as the series with the largest flows. This can be outright investment in other firms but also the retained earnings generated by subsidiaries and other NFCs' investments. The fact that the flow of equity other than quoted shares somehow

---

[56] See European Commission (2015).

tracks the evolution of other loans with about one or one and a half years lag could induce to think that both series are closely interlinked with intragroup operations.

Turning to financial liabilities, although the peak of 2001 was similar in size to the one of 2008 in aggregated terms (Figure A.1), a significant shift in the funding mix is patent (Figure A.3). The former was driven by various components, but mainly other equity while the latter was clearly based on the expansion of bank loans. Between 2006 and 2008, bank loans provided up to 50 percent of the new financing obtained by NFCs, in spite the fact that bank loans represent only 16 percent of the NFCs' outstanding liabilities (Figure 1.5).

These dynamics seem to indicate that banks played a much more prominent role from the supply side in building a bank loan bubble—for instance, by offering loans based on an insufficient assessment of credit quality—than firms from the demand side—there was no special reason for the firms to concentrate their funding on bank loans. Moreover, the analysis of NFCs' assets reveals that firms had accumulated cash buffers, and therefore the sector as a whole did not really need large amounts of credit to finance their normal activities. This unprecedented expansion in loans seems to be connected with an excessive easing in the lending standards required by banks to highly risky firms and projects. New loans were not necessarily used for real investment; to a large extent, they were used for nonproductive financial transactions such as the substitution of older, more expensive debts, buy-back of shares or the acquisition of other companies. Excessive lending to projects of low-quality and high-risk is consistent with the numerous voices asking for balance sheet repair in the banking sector[57] and the high levels of nonperforming loans.

Other sources of finance seem to have been much less affected by the financial crisis than bank loans, including bonds, quoted shares, other equity and loans other than bank loans. The issuance of bonds stands out: with a cumulative net issuance of over €400 billion between 2008 and 2014, NFCs almost doubled their use of bonds as a source of funding in

---

[57] From institutions like the EBA, the IMF and the ECB and authors like Jassaud and Hesse (2013); IMF (2013), Van den End and de Haan (2014), Praet (2014), ECB (2014) or Enria (2013).

terms of stocks from about €630 billion to over €1,050 billion (Section 1.5). Moreover, listed companies issued a significant amount of quoted shares throughout the crisis. However, the main support for financing firms' activities was a continuous inflow of equity other than quoted shares—mainly via retained earnings, but also through injections of fresh new capital. Furthermore, a significant expansion in equity investments outside capital markets is the main driver of the recovery in NFCs funding observed throughout 2015.

As on the assets side, trade credit and other accounts payable—the series "other liabilities"—are highly influenced by the business cycle. The decline which started already in 2006, although still during the expansionary phase, was maybe signaling a change in the cycle. Some firms seemed to be confronted with increasing difficulties to obtain financing, even if this was initially concealed under easy and cheap access to bank credit. Apart from the short recovery in 2010–2011, net flows of other liabilities seem to remain subdued.[58]

Finally, loans other than bank borrowing have held up well in recent years. These loans were an important source of funding throughout the crisis (except for a short spell in 2010). This type of loans, together with retained earnings and equity other than quotes shares, were the main source of fresh financing for firms since the outbreak of the crisis.

Interconnections

The financial positions of the different agents in the economy interconnect them with each other (Section 1.7). Plotting together all the flows generated throughout a certain period of time provides an indication of the relative importance of the different sectors. Similar to what was observed in Figure A.1, the flows mobilized within the financial sector multiply the actual funding provided or received by the real economy (Figure A.4, left-hand panels).

---

[58] The evolution of trade credit and other advances should be interpreted with caution due to its ambivalence. An expansion in such sources of financing may be generated by an increase in activity, but liquidity and solvency problems are also translated into increasing (nonperforming) debts to suppliers and stakeholders in general—for instance, late payment of salaries.

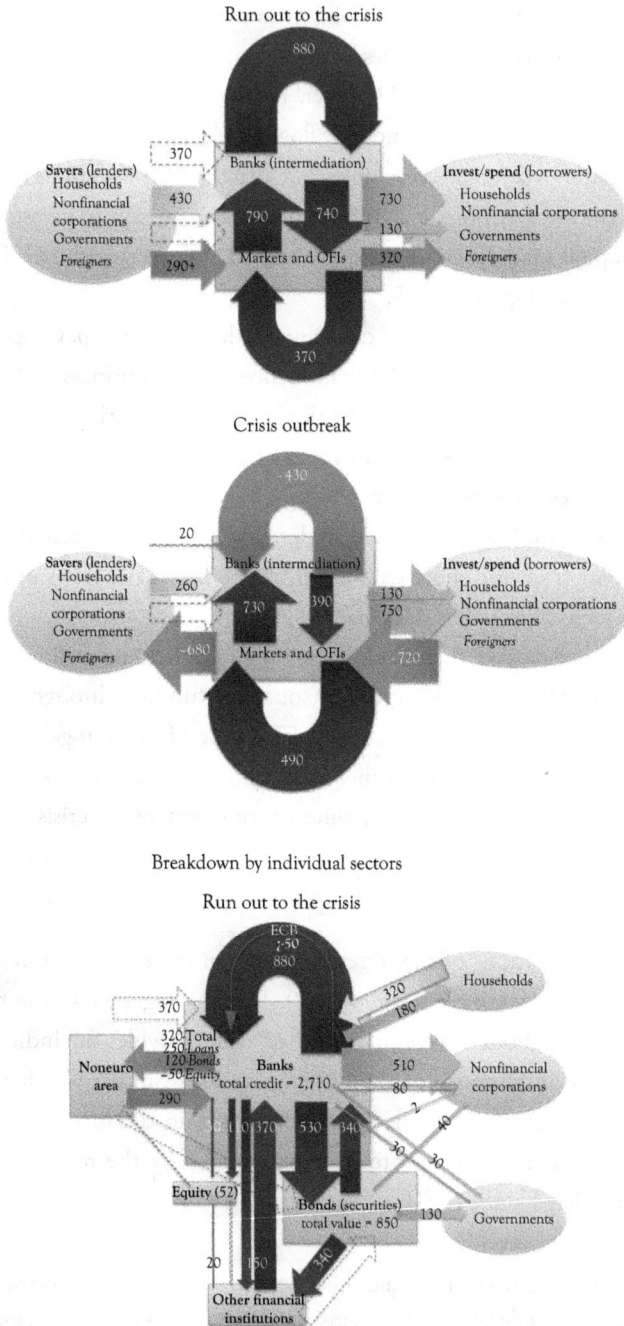

Figure A.4 *Net annual flows between sectors, euro area,*
€ billion   (Continued)

Breakdown by individual sectors

Crisis outbreak

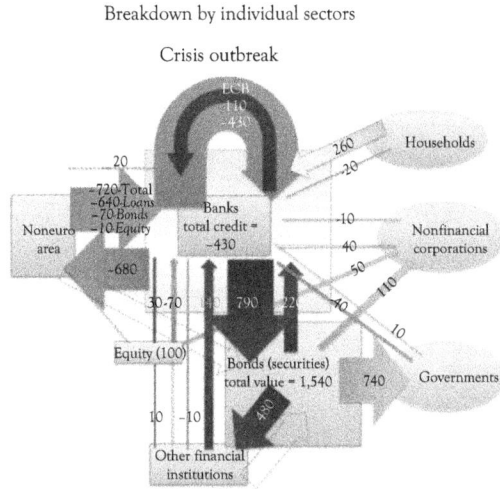

Figure A.4 Net annual flows between sectors, euro area, € billion

Financial transactions between different institutional sectors form a complex network, particularly within the financial sector. Flows within the financial sector are more than twice as large as flows between the financial sector and the real economy. Following the failure of Lehman Brothers in 2008, a reversal in flows from financial institutions is observed. This reflects the drop in confidence and the fact that financial institutions stopped engaging in new contracts and repatriated the funds from previous transactions. The strain experienced by the financial sector ultimately impacted the capacity of the real economy to obtain new funding.

Source: ECB Statistical Data Warehouse and own calculations.

Notes: "Runout to the crisis": the year between October 2007 and September 2008; "Crisis outbreak": the year between October 2008 and September 2009. The width of the arrows is proportional to the size of the flows. Color code: dark grey = interfinancial flows; middle grey = flows to/from nonresidents; light grey: loans or equivalent; white = deposits or equivalent; black = negative flows (redemptions larger than new financial operations); transparent = data not directly available but indirectly estimated. The bowed arrows represent interbank lending and central bank lending provided to banks; on the overview panels, they also include bonds and shares issued by financial institutions and purchased by other financial institutions or loans extended by banks to financial institutions (other than banks). The size of the boxes is proportional to the funds provided by the respective sector during the period. Some bilateral interactions may be missing.

A striking picture appears when the different dynamics occurring during the first year of the crisis are put together (Figure A.4, right-hand panels). The extraordinary repatriation of funds by banks and foreign investors is clearly observed. The illustration also suggests that this was probably the source of the contagion to other sectors in the form of much slimmer flows.

PART B

The Origins of the Financial Crisis

This Part B discusses how imbalances and risks built up over the years and how the financial crisis, which was triggered by the subprime American loans, spread to other jurisdictions and sectors. This process of contagion generated a doom loop of subdued economic growth, weak financial sector, and stressed public accounts. Additional underlying factors such as the financial cycle and the secular rise in income and wealth inequality are discussed in an annex.

CHAPTER 2

Underlying Causes of the Crisis: The Build-Up of Risks and Imbalances

One would like to know "THE" cause of the crisis; however, the run up to the crisis is a complex issue. There is not a unique cause but a series of factors, both at macroeconomic and microeconomic level, that contributed to the build-up of risks and imbalances and drove the expansion of the financial system: abundant global liquidity, rapid credit growth, credits backed by the value of the collateral, high levels of leverage, real estate bubbles, deregulation, financial innovation, technological development, the euro, globalization, supervision too focused on individual institutions and not on the global picture, originate-to-distribute model of lending, complex and opaque financial products like collateralized default obligations (CDOs), conflicts of interest of rating agencies, incentives for short term risk taking, maturity mismatches in banks' balance sheets, and so on. This situation created the breeding ground for the problems to quickly spread throughout the whole financial system through domino effects and feedback loops once a bubble eventually burst.

Why was this allowed to happen or why were measures not taken beforehand to avoid the disaster? The underlying economic expansion and a good economic outlook worked as cushion to hide the build-up of underlying risks, imbalances, and inefficiencies. When the economic conditions weakened, those underlying risks became devastating. This chapter provides some examples of how some flaws in the construction of the euro led to the build-up of macroeconomic imbalances and risks. An annex provides additional information about the role of the business cycle and the rise in inequality.

The Framework of the Single Currency

The creation of the euro in 1999 was one of EU's most far-reaching achievements. The euro became one of Europe's defining symbols at home and across the globe and constitutes a milestone for the economic, social, and environmental well-being of European citizens. However, following the global financial crisis and, in particular the European sovereign debt crisis, the positive mood toward the euro has become more contained.

In macroeconomic terms, the creation of the single currency meant that a central authority, the European Central Bank (ECB), would apply a unique monetary policy to all euro area Member States. To ensure that the monetary policy does not have divergent effects across the single currency area, Member States have to comply with a series of convergence criteria in terms of inflation, public finance, and interest rates before joining the euro.

Fiscal policy—government expenditure and taxation—remained the responsibility of national authorities. Given the safeguard of the large single monetary area, some Member States could be "tempted" to go beyond the limits of sound fiscal policies. To avoid such an undesirable outcome stemming from a moral hazard situation (see Section 1.4), fiscal discipline was ensured through the Stability and Growth Pact (SGP) enshrined in the Treaty on the Functioning of the European Union.

The Pact establishes a cap for public debt and deficit of 60 and 3 percent of gross domestic product (GDP) respectively. The Commission monitors that Member States comply with the SGP.[1]

The Build-Up of Imbalances

In the first years following the adoption of the euro, the economy seemed to perform fine and euro area government bond yields quickly converged (Figure 2.1). However, this convergence was driven more by institutional arrangements than by economic fundamentals. For instance, all euro area

---

[1] For further details about the SGP, see Chapter 8.

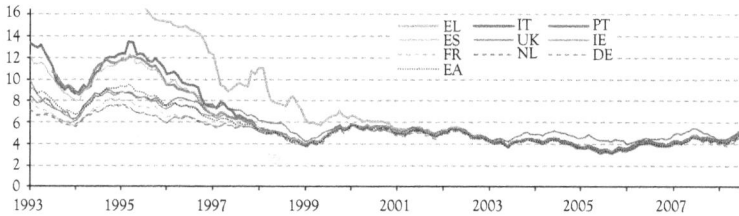

Figure 2.1 Yields on 10-year government bonds, percentage

In the 1990s, governments were paying different interest rates according to the features of their economies. The negotiations toward the single currency and the final adoption of the euro in 1999 led to a convergence across euro area countries in the rates asked by investors for providing funds.

Source: ECB.

government bonds were accepted by the ECB in its repo operation as having the maximum quality, irrespective of actual economic governance and macroeconomic (im)balances. Similarly, banks were not required to back government bonds with capital as they were considered to have the highest quality—in other words, no risk—independently of the issuing country.

Usually, government bond yields provide an indication of the market perception about the risks and economic strength of a country. However, the euro "equalized" all government bonds and eliminated the risk premium. According to government bond yields, the economic performance of Ireland, Italy, or Spain was very similar to the one of Germany, France, or the UK. A selection of indicators including inflation, unit labor cost or current account balance enables to assess if that was really the case.

The ECB aims at keeping inflation below, but close to, 2 percent. Data indicate that average euro area inflation remained around 2 percent since the creation of the euro until the outbreak of the crisis (Figure 2.2, left-hand panel); however, a wide dispersion across individual countries is also observed. Inflation ranged from 1 percent in Germany, Austria, and the Netherlands to 4 or 5 percent in Greece, Ireland, and Spain. Some countries tended to remain on the upper end of the range and some others on the lower end. Consequently, between 2000 and 2008, an

Annual inflation

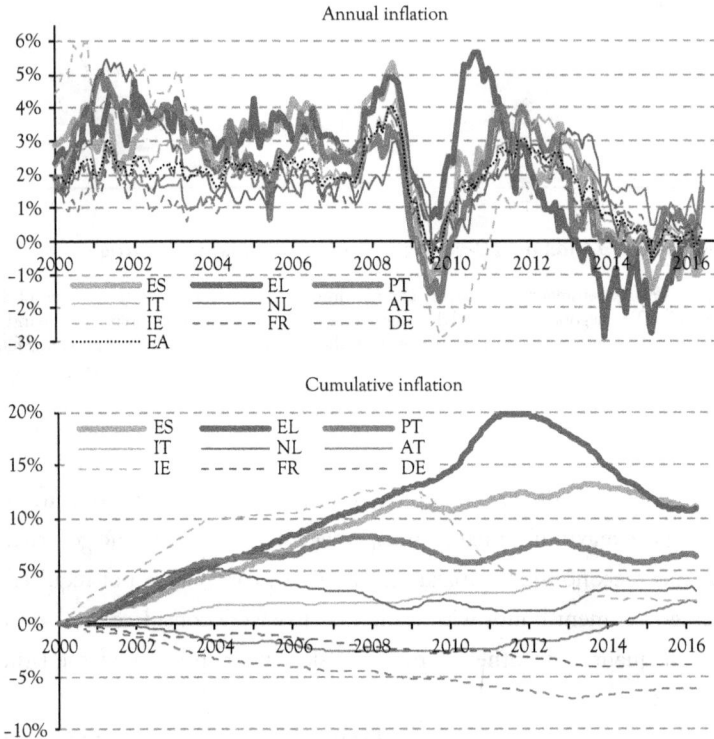

Cumulative inflation

Figure 2.2 Inflation rate, monthly data, percentage

Although annual inflation is volatile, some countries tend to operate with higher inflation than others. Over the years, a large gap is observed in cumulative inflation. This can have significant effects in the international competitive position of euro area countries because they cannot depreciate or appreciate their currency.

Source: ECB and own calculations.

increasing divergence in cumulative inflation is observed across countries (Figure 2.2, right-hand panel).

Higher inflation rates do not necessarily decrease the purchasing power of citizens provided that salaries follow a similar path. However, if the increases in salaries and inflation are not accompanied by an equivalent increase in productivity, the international competitive position of the country will deteriorate with respect to other countries with lower inflation rates.

Annual increase

Cumulative increase

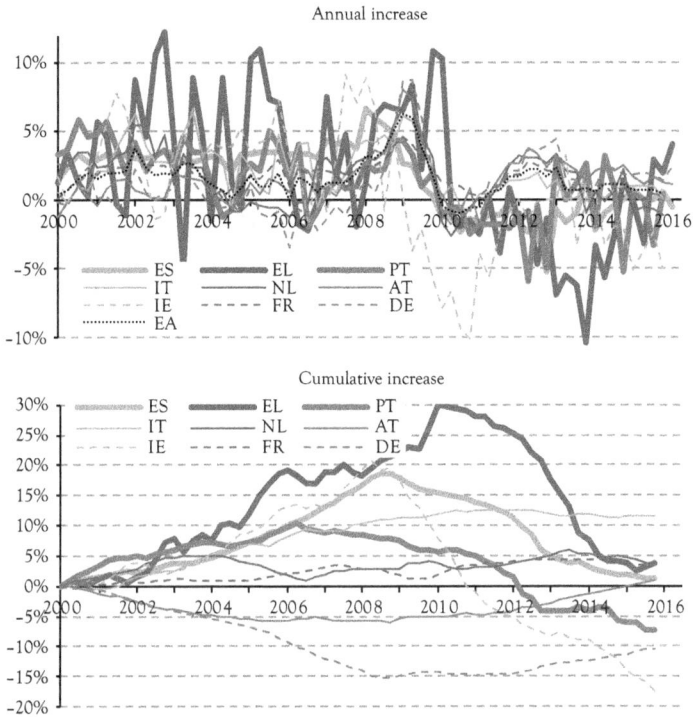

Figure 2.3 Unit labor cost, quarterly data, percentage

As in the case of inflation, an increasing gap is observed in the cumulative increase of unit labor cost across euro area countries. This can be an important source of international economic tensions.

Source: ECB and own calculations.

Similar dynamics are observed in the unit labor cost: by 2008, the labor cost had increased 20 percent more than the euro area average in Ireland, Greece, and Spain while it had decreased in Germany and Austria (Figure 2.3).

High inflation rates and increased unit labor costs deteriorate the international competitiveness of a country resulting in domestic companies encountering increased difficulties to export their products. Moreover, local producers are confronted with imported foreign products with potentially lower prices. Countries with low inflation and low increases in unit labor costs are faced with the opposite situation. These dynamics

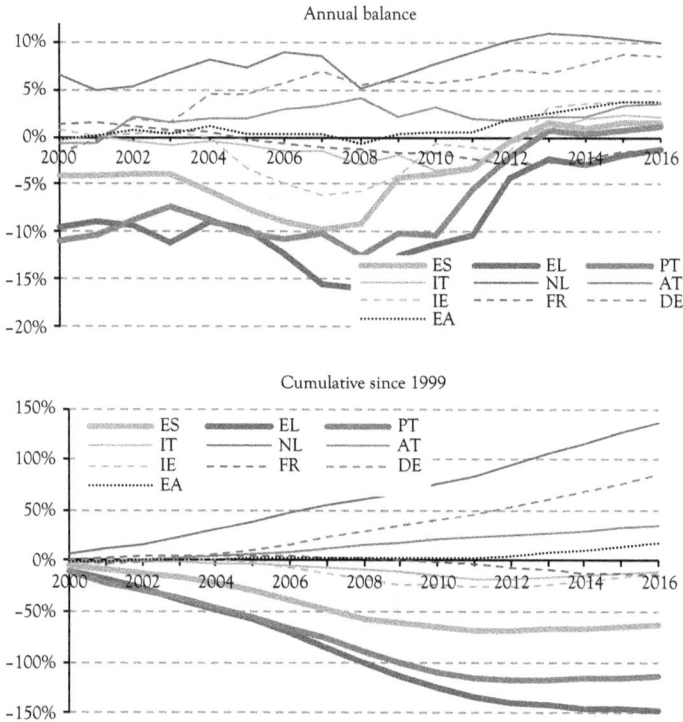

Figure 2.4 Current account balance, percentage of GDP

The diverging international competitive position of the various countries is also observed in the cumulative imbalances in the current account. This can be another source of economic tensions.

Source: ECB and own calculations.

are reflected in the current account balances. By 2008, "deficit" countries—such as Greece, Spain, and Portugal—had accumulated a negative current account balance equivalent to 100 percent of their GDP while "surplus" countries—such as Germany and the Netherlands—had a positive balance of over 60 percent (Figure 2.4).

In Chapter 1, we saw how the different sectors are interconnected and how virtuous and vicious circles can amplify the strengths or weaknesses in an economy. Similar interconnections and feedback effects can also occur at international level. For instance, the dynamics observed in the current account were reinforced through the financing side: Surplus countries found themselves with excess funding, which was lent to deficit countries so that they could finance the purchases of goods and services produced or provided precisely by those surplus countries.

The Spanish housing bubble is an illustration of the interconnections across euro area countries. In 2006, the turnover in the construction sector amounted to €810 billion in the EU as a whole. The turnover of Spanish companies was €280 billion or 35 percent of the total, while the turnover of German and French companies was almost six times lower (€40 billion and €55 billion respectively). The Spanish buildings were equipped with German dishwashers, ovens and other electrical appliances—with brands like Bosch, Miele, or Siemens. Given the buoyant economy, many Spanish workers and entrepreneurs bought new cars, in many cases, from German and French producers—from manufacturers like Renault, Citroën, Volkswagen, Audi, Mercedes, or BMW. Purchasing or building a real estate usually requires obtaining a loan. The Spanish banks were able to provide the financing needed thanks to the cheap interbank credit obtained from German and French banks, which had abundant liquidity due to the buoyance of domestic industries, which were selling their products to Spain. Spanish households were keen to take up loans at considerably lower interest rates than the rates paid before the introduction of the euro (cf. Figure 2.1).

Although in Germany and France there was not such a housing bubble like the one in Spain, the cheap credit generated in surplus countries contributed to the build-up of bubbles in deficit countries. In other words, the financial cycle amplified the economic cycle (see Annex 2.1). Moreover, an important share of the economic dynamism observed in surplus countries stemmed from purchases generated in deficit countries. When problems arise, the agents with a stronger negotiation position— usually the lenders—tend to shift the burden to the other counterpart— the borrowers. However, in reality, there is often a joint responsibility and, given the complex interconnections among economic sectors and countries, a working solution requires a systemic approach. Acknowledging this situation was the first step to foster a robust recovery: The financial and economic crisis required a joint and coordinated reaction at European and global level as individual actions would patently be ineffective.

The Risks Uncovered

Data on inflation, unit labor costs or current account balances demonstrate that the *financial* convergence following the introduction of the euro did not necessarily mean a convergence in the *economic* performance of participating countries. The outbreak of the crisis uncovered the accumulated imbalances and structural weaknesses in some countries. Investors reassessed the specificities of each country and started to ask for differentiated risk premiums on government bonds (Figure 2.5).

In the late 90s, sovereign bond yields converged artificially—due to the new institutional arrangement and somehow disconnected from fundamentals—and did not reflect the actual risks of individual economies. However, it can be argued that the yields observed in 2010 and 2011 were not justified by the actual economic fundamentals either. This amplified reaction was rather signaling high levels of uncertainty.

Conclusions

The crisis revealed the instable equilibrium of the euro area and some structural weaknesses that were concealed by a thriving economy or, at

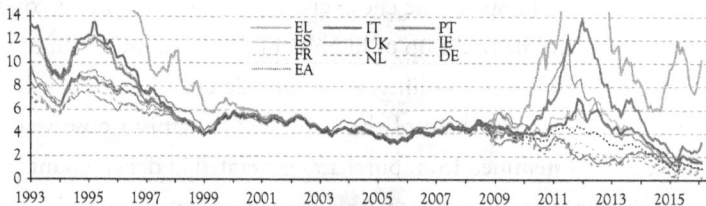

Figure 2.5 Yields on 10-year government bonds, percentage

The crisis uncovered the differences in economic performance across euro area countries. As a consequence, investors asked differentiated borrowing rates to each country. In some cases, borrowing costs became prohibitively expensive. In the early 2000s, yields were not reflecting the fundamental economic features of each country. Similarly, it is also quite likely that the turmoil and panic of the crisis led to rates not entirely consistent with fundamentals. In other words, financial markets do not necessarily operate with perfect rationality and information as in text books.

Source: ECB.

least, by the "great moderation."[2] The European economies implemented a prompt reaction to address the more pressing problems and some structural weaknesses (see Chapters 3 and 4). However, reversing the imbalances accumulated over the years will require some time and should involve both surplus and deficit countries. A comprehensive reaction was needed to avoid that problems emerge again in the future, probably in an amplified form (see Sections C to E). In this chapter, we have seen some of the underlying weaknesses of the European economy; in the next chapter, we discuss how the crisis unfolded. Before that, we briefly discuss in an Annex two additional structural issues that have played a role in the emergence of the crisis: the financial cycle and the raise in inequality.

Annex 2.1 Other Drivers: The Financial Cycle and the Rise in Inequality

Besides the imbalances, two other factors are important underlining forces explaining the origins of the crisis but that initially may have received less attention: the influence of the financial cycle and an increasing unequal distribution of capital and income.

The Financial Cycle

There is an increasing amount of literature interested in analyzing and explaining how the financial cycle matters for systemic banking crises, major macroeconomic dislocations, and serious economic damage.[3] This line of research argues that a focus on the business cycle is not enough to capture the evolution of the global economy in recent years. The financial

---

[2] Note that macroeconomic imbalances are neither a new phenomenon nor exclusive of the euro area. Wikipedia provides a good survey of global imbalances episodes since the 19th century (https://en.wikipedia.org/wiki/Global_imbalances); see also Bracke et al. (2008) or Varoufakis (2011). The great moderation refers to the period starting in the mid-1980s characterized by a reduction in the volatility of business cycle fluctuations (https://en.wikipedia.org/wiki/Great_Moderation).

[3] See, for instance, BIS (2014); Borio (2012); Borio (2013); Drehmann, Borio, and Tsatsaronis (2012).

cycle has become a major driver of the macroeconomy and can help explain the poor growth observed in many advanced economies.

The financial cycle refers to joint fluctuations in a wide set of financial variables. Although there is no consensus on an exact definition, the financial cycles are characterized by four features. First, financial cycles are much longer than business cycles (15 to 20 years for financial cycles compared to 1 to 8 years for business cycles). Second, peaks in the financial cycle are often observed simultaneously to banking crises or significant financial turmoil. Third, the financial cycle is mainly driven by global developments such as global liquidity.[4] and, therefore, it tends to be synchronized across countries. And fourth, an increase in the length and the amplitude of the financial cycle is observed since the early 1980s (Figure A2.1). It has been argued that recent macroeconomic, monetary, and regulatory policy decisions—that is, seemingly stable macroeconomic conditions, an ease monetary stance or financial liberalization—may have disregarded the developments in credit.

The financial cycle seems to be linked to leverage and property prices. Given the differences in duration, the business and the financial cycle may diverge for some time; that is, the financial cycle may seem not to affect the evolution of GDP. However, high private sector debt—generated throughout the financial cycle—end up affecting economic growth—the business cycle—by generating deep recessions when financial booms are exhausted and turned into busts.

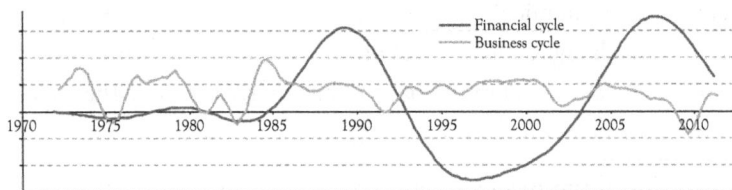

Figure A2.1 The financial and business cycle in the United States

The financial cycle has a much longer duration and a wider amplitude than the business cycle. The change in the business cycle can have strong and long-lasting effects in the business cycle.

Source: Bureau of Economic Analysis; Drehmann, Borio, and Tsatsaronis (2012); and own calculations.

---

[4] See, for instance, Chung et al. (2014).

The financial cycle is also linked to the phenomenon of the debt trap and of "unfinished recessions." Low interest rates may be used to stimulate the economy. However, if the financial cycle is not taken into account, an accommodative monetary policy for too long may encourage the taking-on of even more debt and lead to a larger recession down the road.

The Rise in Inequality

An increasing concentration of capital and income in fewer hands can be mentioned as another important underlying factor of the crisis. This rise in inequality is intertwined with the financial cycle. Indeed, the erosion in the purchasing power of the middle class was compensated by increasing debt levels that allowed to artificially maintain spending. Top income individuals may have promoted the recourse of households to debt—sometimes through intermediaries—as a way of obtaining profitability out of their savings. The eventual bust of the financial bubble led to a significant deceleration in economic activity due to a contraction in consumption, which put it closer to the actual spending capacity of households; the contraction in spending was further exacerbated by the debt overhang confronted by many households.[5]

How does inequality impact economic activity? This is explained by the fact that lower income individuals have a higher propensity to consume than high income individuals. Put it differently, as explained by Hanauer (2012), economic activity or GDP growth is generated by the spending capacity of consumers. While an individual company may prefer the lowest salaries as possible, on aggregate, higher salaries imply larger sales. Already in the early 19th century Henry Ford implemented such a labor philosophy by offering a daily wage of $5 when competitors were paying $2.34. This measure allowed workers to afford the cars they were producing and ultimately had a positive impact on the company and the local economy.[6] This is an example about the interconnections of the sectors in the economy and the potential generation of virtuous circles

---

[5] See also Section 3.1 about subprime borrowers and Section 1.2 about the increasing leverage across sectors.

[6] For further details, see Wikipedia (Henry Ford).

which was discussed in Chapter 1. Examples of authors who argue about how inequality impacts economic growth are Krugman (2013); Mian and Sufi (2014); IMF (2014); Stiglitz (2012); Piketty (2014); Ostry and Berg (2014); and OECD (2014).

Wilkinson (2011) and Wilkinson and Pikett (2009) provide a comprehensive overview of how high levels of inequality are harmful not only for the economy but also for the society. They rely on a wide range of indicators such as physical health, mental health, drug abuse, education, imprisonment, obesity, social mobility, trust and community life, violence, teenage pregnancies, and child well-being.

CHAPTER 3

Triggers

We have just seen how underlying macroeconomic imbalances accumulated over the years. However, problems were deeply rooted in the economy well beyond macroeconomic variables; they were also present in the financial sector. Chapter 3 reviews some of the triggers that led to the global financial crisis and shows how the crisis spread across sectors and throughout the European economy.

The Real Estate Bubble in the United States

The mortgage market developed extraordinarily in the United States over the 2000s. Housing prices had been consistently increasing for years. Financial innovation allowed for many people to buy properties beyond their means. They were also encouraged by the government to do so to boost growth, particularly after 9/11. To achieve that, all kinds of new formulas were created: mortgages with teaser rates—with an initial very low rate—mortgages with balloon payments—a significant amount of capital is left to be paid at maturity—mortgages with negative amortization—with payments smaller than the interest charged and, therefore, with outstanding balance increasing over time—"liar loans"—in which borrower's statements about her income level is not verified by the lender—and others. All these subprime mortgages entailed repeated refinancing. This system ostensibly worked perfectly as long as real estate prices continued to increase. People were happy with their improving standard of living and banks were happy with their increasing income.

The process of securitization completed the system. Sets of mortgage loans were packaged together, securitized, and then sold in the markets. This promised several advantages: the risk could be spread across the world instead of remaining concentrated on the originators—the banks providing the loan to the consumer. Secondly, securitization enabled the creation of tranches: a large proportion of risky loans could become an AAA product of the highest quality, thanks to the stamp of rating agencies.

However, there were important flaws in the system. The originators did not have incentives to control and mitigate the risks and rather focused on increasing their income in the form of fees. Investors around the world were buying AAA-rated American receivables, assuming their top quality without necessarily investigating what was behind. This was definitely not sustainable.

The Model Starts to Totter

To strengthen their resilience and compensate for their intrinsic weak position, banks need to comply with a series of prudential requirements (see Chapter 1). Among other things, banks are required to maintain balanced liquidity positions at the end of each day. Interbank lending markets allow banks to manage their liquidity positions by placing excess liquidity or by obtaining liquidity to compensate for a deficit. In principle, interbank markets are very safe so that prices—or spreads—were traditionally very low.

However, new developments in the U.S. real estate markets were about to change the financial landscape. After peaking in 2006, U.S. housing prices started to decline and thereby threatened the whole construction described in the previous section. Declining prices made the actual value of the portfolios of subprime loans quite uncertain. This raised concerns about the banks holding those portfolios such as Bear Stearns or Merrill Lynch in the United States but also other banks around the globe, from BNP Paribas to Bank of China. This impacted interbank markets: the reluctance of investors with excess liquidity to lend to "suspicious" banks led to an increase in the price and a reduction in the amounts underwritten. Between summer 2007 and summer 2008, the market was embedded with uncertainty about how many toxic assets banks were holding and their actual value. In most cases, those toxic assets represented a fraction of the aggregated banks' balance sheet only; however, some small banks were failing and a few others were bailed-out by public authorities.

In September 2008, the overnight failure of Lehman Brothers, the fourth largest investment bank in the United States, meant a change in

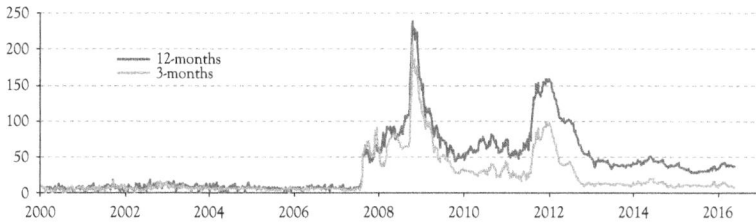

Figure 3.1 Risk perceived in the interbank market, Overnight Indexed Swap (OIS)—Euribor spread, basis points

Interbank markets were traditionally perceived as having very low risk as reflected in the very low spread. The extend of the turmoil generated by the subprime crisis in 2007 and of the panic following the failure of Lehman Brothers in 2008 is reflected in the spikes observed in the spreads. Since then, spread have significantly declined but remain above precrisis levels.

Source: Bloomberg and own calculations.

the game. The market was shocked by the fact that a leading bank had failed; the same fate could fall on any other bank. Confidence evaporated. The immediate soar of spreads in the interbank markets to over 300 basis points (Figure 3.1) signals that no bank was willing to lend to another anymore, in other words, interbank markets dried up.

Support by Central Banks and Governments

The central banks—among them the European Central Bank (ECB)—had to step in to avoid the collapse of the financial system. In its role as a "lender of last resort," the ECB provided as much liquidity as the banks asked for and provisionally substituted interbank markets: the liquidity provided by the ECB to commercial banks soared to over €800 billion at an interest rate that dropped to 1 percent (Figure 3.2).

At the same time, governments implemented a series of policies aiming at making confidence return to markets. Banks would not lend to each other as they feared not to be reimbursed at maturity. Therefore, governments issued guarantees on the bonds of banks in their jurisdictions: in case a bank was unable to reimburse a bond, the State would step in and pay on its behalf. By December 2008, EU States had granted up to €400 billion of guarantees on their banks' bonds (Figure 3.3). These public guarantees improved investors' confidence as reflected in declining

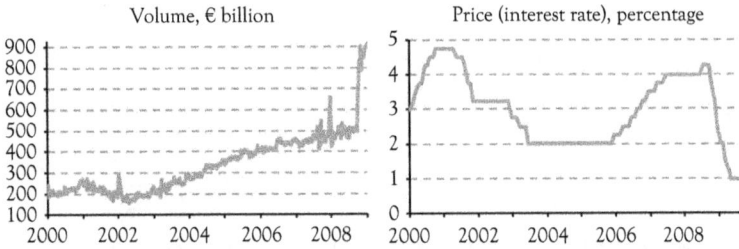

Figure 3.2 Liquidity provided to euro area banks by the ECB

The European Central Bank reacted to the outbreak of the crisis by offering increasing amounts of liquidity at a lower cost to banks.

Source: ECB.

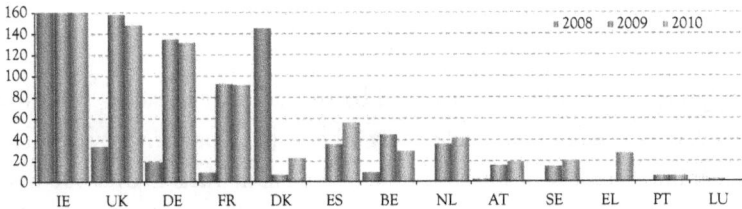

Figure 3.3 State guaranteed bonds, € billion

In order to restore confidence on financial institutions, governments guaranteed the bonds issued by their banks.

Source: European Commission.

Notes: Guarantees granted by the Irish government reached a peak of 285 billion in 2009 because of the blank guarantee.

spreads (Figure 3.1) and in the reactivation of the volumes in interbank markets. The United Kingdom, Germany, and France were the countries with the largest support to their financial systems in the initial phases of the crisis.[1]

In parallel to the financial turmoil of 2008–2010, economic activity started to slow down and unemployment started to rise (Figures 1.19 to 1.21). The excesses and imbalances accumulated over the years across EU countries started to surface and increasing numbers of households and

[1] Ireland and Denmark represent specific cases as the government granted a blank guarantee to all the bonds issued by the banks under their jurisdictions (and not only guarantees to new issuances as in the other countries).

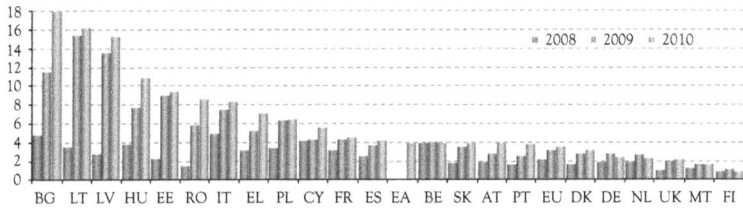

Figure 3.4 Nonperforming loans, percentage

The slowdown in real economy—and the excessive ease in the provision of credit in the pass—translated into increasing nonperforming loans, particularly in certain countries.

Source: ECB.

Notes: Guarantees granted by the Irish government reached a peak of 285 billion in 2009 because of the blank guarantee.

companies started to have difficulties to repay their credits. Confronted with losses and more aware of the (low) creditworthiness of potential borrowers, banks restricted the provision of new loans. All of this pushed up the level of nonperforming loans (Figure 3.4) and further eroded bank income on top of the contagion stemming from the U.S. subprime market.[2]

A potential problem—confidence—was materializing into actual losses. Therefore, governments also stepped in to directly inject capital on the many banks that have suffered massive losses. By December 2012, EU Member States had injected more than €300 billion of public funds into the banking system (Figure 3.5).

Erosion in Public Finances and the Sovereign Crisis

The public interventions helped stabilize financial markets; however, they also eroded public accounts. By 2011, public debt in many countries had gone well beyond the 60 percent threshold established by the Stability and Growth Pact (Figure 3.6).

---

[2] The discussion about the reaction in the United States, which was also significant, goes beyond the scope of this book. The reader can consult, for instance, Krugman (2013); Mian and Sufi (2014); Stiglitz (2010); or the final report of the U.S. Financial Crisis Inquiry Commission (Angelides et al. 2011).

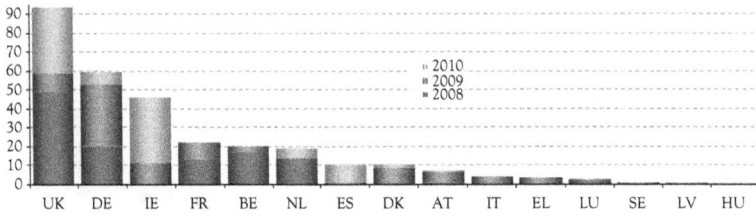

Figure 3.5 *Capital injected in banks by public authorities, € billion*

Banks incurred in large losses bringing them, in some cases, to or close to insolvency. No private investors were willing to support such financial institutions, so that governments stepped in and bail out financial institutions through large public capital injections.

Source: European Commission.

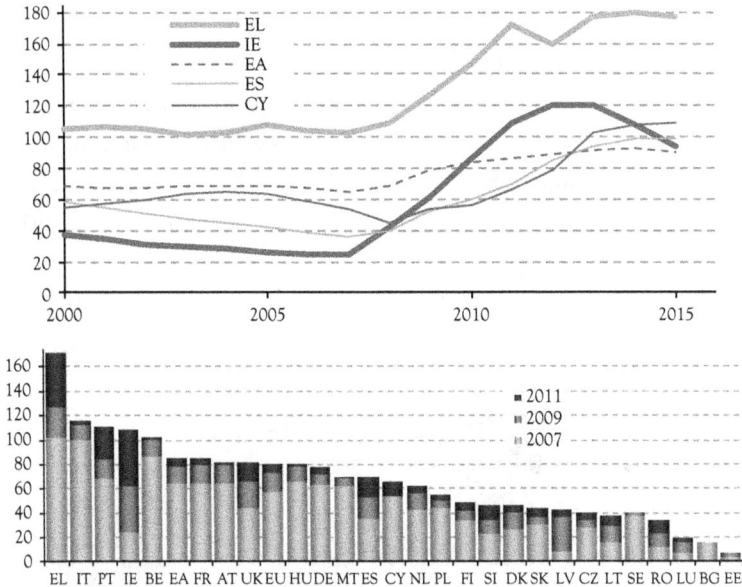

Figure 3.6 *Public debt, percentage of GDP*

The automatic stabilizers—for example, unemployment benefits—and the funding injected to support financial institutions translated in increasing amounts of public debt.

Source: Eurostat.

With the introduction of the euro, government bond yields converged across countries (Chapter 2). Although the response to the crisis was coordinated at European level, each country remained responsible for its own banking system. On the wake of the erosion in public finances, investors

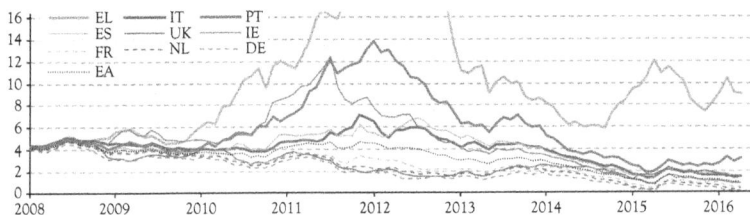

Figure 3.7 Yields on 10-year government bonds, percentage

The deterioration in the fiscal position of some countries and in their economic performance translated into increasing government bond yields.

Source: ECB.

realized that not all the countries were the same and asked for increasing interest rates to lend money to the weakest countries (Figure 3.7). This in itself could only worsen the situation.

Transmission to the Real Economy and Second Round Effects

The problems in the financial sector forced governments to step in and put pressure on public finances. Tighter lending conditions confronted by governments impacted back on national banks: Investors asked increasing interest rates for lending money to banks in the weakest countries. Indeed, high correlations between sovereign credit default swaps (CDSs) and bank CDSs are observed within the countries under fiscal stress independently of the strength of the banks themselves (Figure 3.8). Increasing CDSs signal increasing perceived risks and, therefore, banks are confronted with increasing cost of funding.

Moreover, banks translated their increasing funding costs to their customers by asking for higher interest rates on their (new) loans and by restricting the effective amounts lent. In other words, banks in countries under fiscal stress were unable to translate the declines in the ECB rates (Figure 3.2) into the rates charged to customers (Figure 3.9). The difficulties in the real economy fed back to the financial sectors through households and corporations that became unable to repay their credits (Figure 3.4).

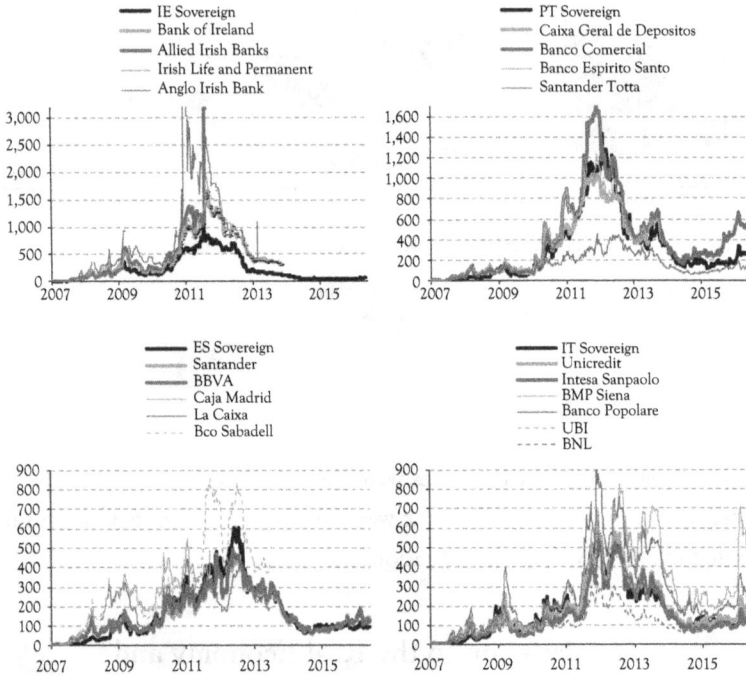

Figure 3.8 CDS spreads, 5 years, selection of countries

The deterioration in government finance and the economic performance impacted not only the risk premium of governments, but also translated to their national banks as reflected in increasing CDS spreads.

Source: Bloomberg.

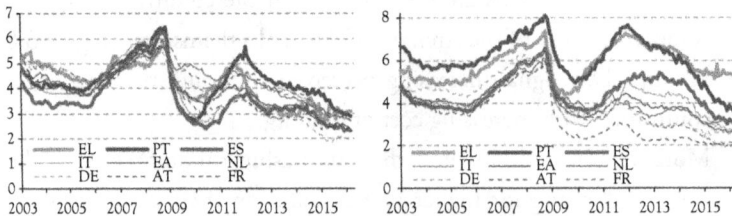

Figure 3.9 Interest rates on new loans, percentage

Banks experiencing difficulties to finance themselves passed their increasing costs to their customers in the form of higher lending rates. Other banks experienced less constrains and reduced their lending rates more in line with the declines in the policy rate. As a consequence, a large dispersion in lending rates was observed across the countries sharing the single currency.

Source: ECB.

Conclusion

In Chapter 1, we discussed the interdependence of all the agents in an economy. In this chapter, we show how, following some triggering effects, the underlining structural weaknesses embarked the economy into a vicious cycle: a slowing economy eroded the bank and public accounts and fed back into an even slower growth (Figure 3.10). As it will be shown throughout the Volume II, the goal of public authorities evolved from addressing isolated bouts of problems to stop the vicious cycle with a more systematic approach.

Throughout this Volume I, we have reviewed the structure of the European financial sector, the factors leading to the global economic and financial crisis as well as how the crisis unfolded. Volume II will present how public authorities, both at national and EU level, responded to the crisis on a temporary basis to address some urgent and *ad hoc* issues as well as on a permanent basis to tackle structural problems in certain policy areas.

The response was orchestrated from many different fronts. The emergency financial support provided to both financial institutions and to sovereigns under stress is discussed in Part C. These efforts aimed at stabilizing the system through a sort of fire brigade. Fixing the flaws from a more structural perspective is discussed in Parts D (dealing with the regulatory reform) and E (discussing macroeconomic policies).

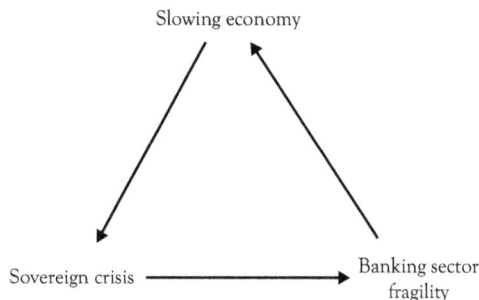

Figure 3.10 Feedback loop

The financial difficulties in the financial sector translated into the real economy and public finances and fed back to the financial sector in a sort of doom loop.

Source: Own elaboration.

Finally, Part F closes Volume II and the book by summarizing the different pieces of the policy reaction to the crisis and how they all fit together. It also reviews the future vision the European Union would like to head to and briefly discusses the potential challenges the European Union is likely to face in its way towards achieving that vision.

Acronyms

Table A1: General acronyms

ABS	Asset-backed security
AD	Accounting Directive
AGS	Annual growth survey
AIF	Alternative investment fund
AIFMD	Alternative Investment Fund Managers Directive
AMLD	Anti-money Laundering Directive
AMR	Alert mechanism report
ATM	Automatic teller machine
BIS	Bank of International Settlements
BoP	Balance of payments
BRRD	Bank recovery and resolution Directive
BSR	Bank Structural Reform
CBPP	Covered bonds purchase program
CACs	Collective action clauses
CCD	Consumer Credit Directive
CCI	Convergence and competitiveness instrument
CCPs	Central counterparty clearing houses
CDOs	Colletarized debt obligations
CDSs	Credit default swaps
CMU	Capital Markets Union
CRA	Credit rating agency
CRR/CRD IV	Capital Requirements Regulation/Directive
CSDR	Central Securities Depositories Regulation
CSPP	Corporate sector purchase program
CSRs	Country-specific recommendations
DG COMP	European Commission Directorate-General for Competition
DG ECFIN	European Commission Directorate-General for Economic and Financial Affairs
DG FISMA	European Commission Directorate-General for Financial Stability, Financial Services and Capital Markets Union

DG JUST	European Commission Directorate-General for Justice and Consumers
DGSD	Deposit Guarantee Scheme Directive
EA	Euro area
EBA	European Banking Authority
EBRD	European Bank for Reconstruction and Development
ECA	European Court of Auditors
ECB	European Central Bank
ECJ	European Court of Justice
EDIS	European Deposit Insurance Scheme
EDP	Excessive deficit procedure
EERP	European economy recovery plan
EFSF	European Financial Stability Facility
EFSI	European Fund for Strategic Investment
EFSM	European Financial Stability Mechanism
EIB	European Investment Bank
EIOPA	European Insurance and Occupational Pensions Authority
EIP	Excessive imbalance procedure
ELA	Emergency liquidity assistance
ELTIF	European long-term Investment Fund
EMIR	Regulation on OTC derivatives, central counterparties and trade repositories
EMU	Economic and monetary union
EONIA	Euro overnight index average
ESAs	European Supervisory Authorities
ESFS	European System of Financial Supervision
ESM	European Stability Mechanism
ESMA	European Securities and Markets Authority
ESRB	European Systemic Risk Board
EU	European Union
EuSEF	European Social Entrepreneurship Funds
EuVECA	European Venture Capital Fund
FAP	Financial assistance programme
FICOD	Financial Conglomerates Directive
FSB	Financial Stability Board
FTT	Financial Transaction Tax

GDP	Gross domestic product
GLF	Greek loan facility
ICPFs	Insurance corporations and pension funds
IDD	Insurance Distribution Directive
IDR	In-depth review
IMD	Insurance Mediation Directive
IMF	International Monetary Fund
IORP	Institutions of Occupational Retirement Pensions
IOSCO	International Organization of Securities Commissions
IT	Information technology
LTROs	Longer-term refinancing operations
MAD/R	Market Abuse Regulation and Criminal Sanctions Directive
MCD	Mortgage Credit Directive
MFIs	Monetary and financial institutions
MiFID II/R	Markets in Financial Instruments Directive and Regulation
MIP	Macroeconomic imbalances procedure
MMF	Money Market Fund
MS	Member State
NFCs	Non-financial corporations
NPL	Non-performing loan
OFIs	Other financial institutions
OMTs	Outright monetary transactions
PAD	Payments Account Directive
PD	Prospectus Directive
PRIIPs	Packaged retail and insurance-based investment products
PSD	Payment Services Directive
PSI	Private sector involvement
PSPP	Public sector purchase program
QE	Quantitative easing
RoW	Rest of the world
R&D	Research and technological development
SEPA	Single Euro Payments Area
SFTR	Securities Financing Transactions Regulation
SGP	Stability and growth pact
SMEs	Small and medium-sized enterprises

SMP	Securities markets program
SRF	Single Resolution Fund
SFTR	Securities Financing Transactions Regulation
SRM	Single Resolution Mechanism
SRSS	Structural Reform Support Service
SSM	Single Supervisory Mechanism
SSR	Short Selling Regulation
STS	Simple, transparent and standardized securitization
TD	Transparency Directive
UCITS	Undertakings for collective investment in transferable securities
U.K.	The United Kingdom
U.S.	The United States of America

Table A2: Acronyms for EU countries and regions

EU	European Union
EA	Euro area
AT	Austria
BE	Belgium
BG	Bulgaria
CY	Cyprus
CZ	Czech Republic
DE	Germany
DK	Denmark
EE	Estonia
EL	Greece
ES	Spain
FI	Finland
FR	France
HR	Croatia
HU	Hungary
IE	Ireland
IT	Italy
LT	Lithuania
LU	Luxembourg
LV	Latvia
MT	Malta
NL	Netherlands
PL	Poland
PT	Portugal
RO	Romania
SE	Sweden
SI	Slovenia
SK	Slovakia
UK	United Kingdom

References

Part A

Abbassi, P., and Schnabel, I. 2009. "Contagion among interbank money markets during the subprime crisis." *Working Paper*. Johannes Gutenberg University Mainz.

Adrian, T., and Shin, H. S. 2010. *The Changing Nature of Financial Intermediation and the Financial Crisis of 2007–09*. Staff Report no. 439. Federal Reserve Bank of New York.

Arrow, K. J., P. W. Anderson, and D. Pines, eds. 1988. "The Economy as an Evolving Complex System." In *Proceedings of the Evolutionary Paths of the Global Economy Workshop Held September*, 1987 in Santa Fe, New Mexico. Redwood City, California: Addison-Wesley Pub. Co.

Brunnermeier, M. K., and Schnabel, I. 2015. Bubbles and Central Banks: Historical Perspectives.

Buttiglione, L., Lane, P. R., Reichlin, L., and Reinhart, V. (eds.) 2014. *Deleveraging? What Deleveraging? The 16th Geneva Reports on the World Economy.* International Center for Monetary and Banking Studies and Centre for Economic Policy Research.

Castrén, O., and Rancan, M. 2013. "Macro-networks. An application to the Euro area financial accounts." *Working Paper*, No. 1510. European Central Bank.

Cochrane, J. H. 2014. "Toward a run-free financial system." In Baily, M. N., and Taylor, J. B. (eds.). *Across the Great Divide: New Perspectives on the Financial Crisis*. Hoover Press.

Cœuré, B. 2013. *The implications of bail-in rules for bank activity and stability.* Opening speech at Conference on "Financing the recovery after the crisis– the roles of bank profitability, stability and regulation." Bocconi University. Milan. 30 September.

Enria, A. 2013. *Completing the repair of the EU banking sector*. Speech at Oliver Wyman Institute Conference "The emerging structure of the financial services industry." London. 1 October.

European Central Bank. 2014. *Banking Structure Report*. October.

European Commission. 2011. *Impact assessment for the Recommendation on access to a basic payment account*. SEC(2011) 906.

European Commission. 2015. *European Financial Stability and Integration Review—EFSIR. April 2015.*

Fender, I and Lewrick, U. 2015. "Shifting tides – market liquidity and market-making in fixed income instruments." *BIS Quarterly Review March 2015.*

FSB (Financial Stability Board (2015): *Global Shadow Banking Monitoring Report 2015.*

Garriga, C., Kydland F. E., and Sustek, R. 2016. *Mortgages and Monetary Policy.*

Giovannini, A., Mayer, C., Micossi, S., Di Noia, C. Onada M. et al. 2015. *Restarting European long-term investment finance. A green paper discussion document.* Centre for Economic Policy Research.

Gorton, G., and Metrick, A. 2012. "Securitized banking and the run on repo." *Journal of Financial Economics*, 104, no. 3, pp. 425–51.

Haldane, A. G. 2015. *On microscopes and telescopes.* Speech at the Lorentz centre workshop on socio-economic complexity. Leiden, Netherlands. 27 March.

Hautony, G., and Héamz J. C. 2014. *How to measure interconnectedness between banks, insurers and financial conglomerates?* Autorité de Contrôle Prudentiel et de Résolution (France).

Hope, K., and Atkins R. 2014: "Greece cuts state wage bill by more than a third." *Financial Times.* 24 July.

International Monetary Fund. 2013. *European Union. Financial System Stability Assessment.* 22 February.

Jassaud, N., and Hesse, H. 2013. *Balance-sheet repairs in European banks.* VoxEU, 13 April.

Jorda, O., Schularick, M., and Taylor A. M. 2015: "Leveraged Bubbles." *NBER Working Paper*, No. 21486.

Khalip, A., and Gonçalves, S. 2013: *Portugal court rejects some government austerity measures.* Reuters. 5 April.

Krugman, P. 2013. *End this depression now!* New York: Norton.

Kuehnhausen, F., and Stieber, H. W. 2014. "Determinants of Capital Structure in Non-Financial Companies." *SSRN Working Paper*, No. 2410741.

OECD (Organisation for Economic Co-operation and Development). 2016. *New Approaches to Economic Challenges. Insights into Complexity and Policy.* Available at: www.oecd.org/naec/Insights%20into%20Complexity%20 and%20Policy.pdf.

Pagano, M., and M., S. Langfield, V. Acharya, A. Boot, M. Brunnermeier, C. Buch, M. Hellwig, A. Sapir, I. van den Burg (Chair) 2014. *Is Europe overbanked?* Advisory Scientific Committee of the ESRB.

Papadimas, L. 2014. *Top Greek court reverses some troika-mandated wage cuts.* Reuters. 22 January.

Praet, P. 2014. *Repairing the bank lending channel: the next steps.* Speech at European Macro Conference organised by Credit Suisse. London. 17 November.

Reinhart, C. M., Reinhart, V., and Rogoff, K. 2015: "Dealing with Debt." *Journal of International Economics*, Volume 96, Supplement 1, pp. S43–S55.

Reinhart, C. M., and Rogoff, K. S. 2011. *This time is different. Eight centuries of financial folly.* Princeton University Press.

Roxburgh, C., Lund, S., Daruvala, T., Manyika, J., Dobbs, R. et al. 2012. *Debt and deleveraging: Uneven progress on the path to growth.* McKinsey Global Institute.

Stephanie, L., and Rogoff, K. 2015. "Secular stagnation, debt overhang and other rationales for sluggish growth, six years on." *BIS Working Paper 482.*

Van den End, J. W., and J. de Haan. 2014. *Europe's banking problem through the lens of secular stagnation.* VoxEU. 28 March.

Varoufakis, Y. 2011. *The Global Minotaur: America, The True Origins of the Financial Crisis and the Future of the World Economy.* Zed Books.

Villar Burke, J. 2016. "Impact of Loan Contract Characteristics on Monetary Transmission and Consumer Rent," *SSRN Working Paper*, No. 2535571.

Part B

Angelides, P., B. Thomas, B. Born, B. Georgiou, B. Graham, H.H. Murren, J.W. Thompson. 2011. *The Financial Crisis Inquiry Report.* U.S. Government Printing Office. Available at: www.fcic.gov/REPORT.

BIS (Bank of International Settlements). 2014. "Debt and the Financial Cycle: Domestic and Global." BIS Annual Report—Chapter IV.

Borio, C. 2012. "The Financial Cycle and Macroeconomics: What Have We Learnt?" *Working Papers*, No. 395. Basel: Bank of International Settlements.

Borio, C. February 2, 2013. "Macroeconomics and the Financial Cycle: Hamlet Without the Prince?" VoxEU.org.

Bracke, T., M. Bussière, M. Fidora, and R. Straub. 2008. "A Framework for Assessing Global Imbalances." Occasional Paper Series, No. 78. Frankfurt: European Central Bank.

Credit. Princeton, NJ: Princeton University Press.

Chung, K., J.E. Lee, E. Loukoianova, H. Park, and H.S. Shin. 2014. "Global Liquidity through the Lens of Monetary Aggregates". Working Paper, No. 14/9. Washington: International Monetary Fund.

Drehmann, M., C. Borio, and K. Tsatsaronis. 2012. "Characterising the Financial Cycle: Don't Lose Sight of the Medium Term." Working Papers, No. 380. Basel: Bank of International Settlements.

Hanauer, N. 2012. "Rich people don't create jobs". TED Talk. Available at: https://www.youtube.com/watch?v=CKCvf8E7V1g.

IMF (International Monetary Fund). 2014. "Inequality Seriously Damages Growth". *IMF Survey Magazine*, 12 April.

Krugman, P. 2013. *End this Depression Now!* New York: Norton.

Mian, A., and A. Sufi. 2014. *House of Debt. How They (and You) Caused the Great Recession, and How We Can Prevent It from Happening Again.* Chicago: The University of Chicago Press.

Stiglitz, J.E. 2010. *Freefall: America, Free Markets, and the Sinking of the World Economy.* New York: W. W. Norton and Company.

Varoufakis, Y. 2011. *The Global Minotaur. America, the True Causes of the Financial Crisis and the Future of the World Economy.* London: Zed Books.

Additional Recommended Reading

Calomiris, C.W., and S.H. Haber. 2014. *Fragile by Design. The Political Origins of Banking Crises and Scarce.*

Frank, R. H., and P. J. Cook. 1996. *The winner-take-all society: Why the few at the top get so much more than the rest of us.* Penguin.

Galbraith, J. K. 2012. *Inequality and instability: A study of the world economy just before the Great Crisis.* Oxford University Press.

Lewis, M. 2014. *Flash Boys. A Wall Street revolt.* W. W. Norton & Company.

Obstfeld, M., and K. Rogoff. 2009. "Global Imbalances and the Financial Crisis: Products of Common Causes." *CEPR Discussion Paper No. DP7606.*

OECD (Organisation for Economic Co-operation and Development). December 2014. "Does Income Inequality Hurt Economic Growth." Focus on Inequality and Growth.

Ostry, J.D., and A.G. Berg. September 2014. "Measure to Measure." *Finance and Development.* International Monetary Fund.

Pelkmans, J. 2006. *European Integration. Methods and Economic Analysis.* Pearson Education.

Piketty, T. 2014. *The Capital in the Twenty-First Century.* Cambridge, MA: Belknap Press.

Rajan, R.G. 2011. *Fault Lines. How Hidden Fractures Still Threaten the World Economy.* Princeton, NJ: Princeton University Press.

Sorkin A.R. 2010. *Too Big to Fail. Inside the Battle to Save Wall Street.* London: Penguin Books.

Stiglitz, J.E. 2010. *Freefall: America, Free Markets, and the Sinking of the World Economy.* New York: W. W. Norton and Company.

Stiglitz, J.E. 2012. *The Price of Inequality.* New York: W. W. Norton and Company.

Turner, A. 2013. *Debt, Money and Mephistopheles—How Do We Get Out of this Mess.* Financial Services Authority.

Wilkinson, R. 2011. "How Economic Inequality Harms Societies". *TED Talk.* Available at: www.ted.com/talks/richard_wilkinson?language=en

Wilkinson, R., and K. Pickett. 2009. *The Spirit Level: Why More Equal Societies Almost Always Do Better.* London: Allen Lane.

Wolf, M. 2014. *The Shifts and the Shocks. What We've Learned—and Have Still to Learn—from the Financial Crisis.* London: Penguin Press.

Index

OTHER TITLES IN OUR FINANCE AND FINANCIAL MANAGEMENT COLLECTION

John A. Doukas, Old Dominion University, Editor

- *Capital Budgeting* by Sandeep Goel
- *Online Marketing to Investors: How to Develop Effective Investor Relations* by Daniel R. Valentine
- *Essentials of Retirement Planning: A Holistic Review of Personal Retirement Planning Issues and Employer-Sponsored Plans, Third Edition* by Eric J. Robbins
- *Redefining Shareholder Value: Demystifying the Valuation Myth* by Mariana Schmid and Milan Frankl
- *Financial Ratios* by Sandeep Goel
- *Financial Services Sales Handbook: A Professionals Guide to Becoming a Top Producer* by Clifton T. Warren
- *Money Laundering and Terrorist Financing Activities: A Primer on Avoidance Management for Money Managers* by Milan Frankl and Ayse Ebru Kurcer
- *Introduction to Foreign Exchange Rates, Second Edition* by Thomas J. O'Brien
- *Rays of Research on Real Estate Development* by Jaime Luque
- *Weathering the Storm: The Financial Crisis and the EU Response, Volume II: The Response to the Crisis* by Javier Villar Burke

Announcing the Business Expert Press Digital Library

Concise e-books business students need for classroom and research

This book can also be purchased in an e-book collection by your library as

- a one-time purchase,
- that is owned forever,
- allows for simultaneous readers,
- has no restrictions on printing, and
- can be downloaded as PDFs from within the library community.

Our digital library collections are a great solution to beat the rising cost of textbooks. E-books can be loaded into their course management systems or onto students' e-book readers.
The **Business Expert Press** digital libraries are very affordable, with no obligation to buy in future years. For more information, please visit **www.businessexpertpress.com/librarians**. To set up a trial in the United States, please email **sales@businessexpertpress.com**.